D0112365

The ART of Feeding HEROES

Leading from the Inside Out

The ART of Feeding HEROES

Jean-Marie Jobs

THREE UNCLES
PUBLISHING

Published by Three Uncles Publishing
P.O. Box 150419
San Rafael CA 94915

ISBN: 978-0-9961251-1-6

"Everyday courage has few witnesses.
But yours is no less noble because no drum beats for you
and no crowds shout your name."

Robert Louis Stevenson

Contents

Preface

Our lives are a mixture, a combination of pain and joy, suffering and moments of wonder. Growing up in a home where violence and often abuse was mixed with art, music and creativity, I sought refuge in books. Always a voracious reader, I consumed fiction, non-fiction, philosophy, and religion. The escape from reality was equally as important as my exploration of it.

I grew up in Irving, Texas. Being born in 1962, most of my childhood was in the late 60s and early 70s. We grew up Catholic so going to church was a routine until leaving home for college. I applied to several universities, my main goal being to get as far away from home as possible. In the fall of 1981, I took off for the East Coast.

Once I left home, I found other means of both escape and exploration, most of them incongruent with my Catholic upbringing. I remember thinking as I boarded the plane to D.C. for my freshman year at Georgetown University "No one knows me. I can completely reinvent myself." That would have been possible if only I had really understood myself in the first place.

After two years there, I was financially unable to continue paying tuition and moved to New York City. My dad and his new wife lived there and it seemed like a great place to start over – again. Still, I found myself in repeating patterns of behavior: unhealthy relationships, excessive drinking, lying. In 1986, I got pregnant. It took me a few months to realize what was happening. I thought I had an ulcer or stomach flu. The news was a wake-up call of sorts. I did stop drinking. However, my relationship to relationships did not really change.

After an unsuccessful attempt to work it out with my son's father,
I started looking elsewhere. I got engaged to my high school sweetheart,
who was attending law school in California and moved to the Bay Area.
Another chance to start over!

Again, my blindness to my own strategies sabotaged the possibility
of having anything new. After we broke up, I just decided to move
in with my next boyfriend and get married to him. That lasted almost
6 months before I moved out, convinced it was about him. Time to
start over again. Are you seeing a pattern here? I didn't see it—and
wouldn't for another few years.

I poured all of my energy into my son and my work. Work was easy
to manage, to find ways to create success. After 3 years with the company
I was working with in San Francisco, it dawned on me that something
was wrong. I was getting raises and promotions every 6 months but
my personal life was still a series of bad choices and broken relationships.
One day, I asked my friend Lynne "What is wrong with me? I know
I'm not stupid, I go to school and make 'A's, I come to work and get
raises and promotions but somehow, in my personal life, I can't seem
to make a good decision. What am I missing?" She sat back in her chair
and said "Well, you're the type of person who does really well when
you understand the rules of the game. I don't think you really understand
the game of life." "OK, great, give me the rule book!" I replied. She
responded "Let's talk again tomorrow."

The next day, she invited me to drive up to Santa Rosa over the
weekend, visit her family and go to church with them. I did.
I don't remember much about the service or the message that Sunday.
I guess I didn't really come to hear it. Although I didn't realize it,
I came to meet Jesus.

Now if you are tempted to stop reading here and toss this book, wait. Don't miss the transformation, the process which makes starting over again real instead of imaginary.

My life did change, not all at once and certainly not perfectly, if such a thing exists. That same year, I met the man who is now my husband. Initially, he did not show up on my 'radar' as a potential mate. But hey, my radar had never worked well so who was I kidding to adhere to it like the law? Loving him and being loved by him transformed (and continues to transform) my definition of love. It occurred to me after about six months of marriage, my entire framework for love was based on a mixture of narcissism and false assumptions. We were married in 1993 and recently celebrated 25 years.

Yes, I believe in Jesus, in a relationship with God and His Spirit. That does not make me a bigot or a conservative or a liberal or an extremist. I also love neuroscience, biology, philosophy, psychology and multi-cultural learning. I enjoy being challenged, stretched and inspired. My exploration of what it means to be human and be in relationship is continually expanding around the axis of Love.

So read, please, enjoy. Allow yourself to be challenged. Notice if you automatically discount the wisdom of science or of the Bible or of philosophy or of ancient wisdom or of great business minds. And relax. It is possible to try on something that seems the opposite of what you currently believe, without losing your belief. Maybe the bench that truth sits on is bigger than you think.

Introduction

Why am I doing this? While writing this book, I asked myself this question regularly. *What is the bigger purpose, the motivation, the vision?* This question became an anchor in my storm of emotional ups and downs. The process of putting my thoughts, experiences, and emotions out for the world to see felt vulnerable. Sometimes it seemed as if there were no words and other times, too many words. At times, the writing process was pure frustration. At other times, it was like driving around singing along to the radio with the windows down on a summer day. What I realized in this process has gone well beyond my feelings, insecurities, and frustrations. I became intimately connected to my purpose, my WHY in life. I have a big WHY. I am committed to living my legacy in every interaction. My legacy is letting people know they are loved, they are worth fighting for, that hope lives, and love reigns. That is a tall order for a girl from a small town in the big state of Texas!

Since 1996, I have had the joy and privilege of doing transformational work in both faith-based non-profit and corporate sectors. This book is a collection of what I have learned, unlearned and experienced. I have trained thousands of people. I have worked with everyone from executives of Fortune 100 companies to orphans in third world countries. Wherever I go, I find the main conversations and questions people live in are essentially the same ones I ask myself: *What do I have to contribute, do I matter,* and *how can I make a difference?*

In the context of training, people typically come together to have something new birthed in their lives, organizations, or communities.

I have been marked by people's passion, care, courage, and risk and have seen these same marks made in the lives of others. I have learned that every transformation in someone's life is an exchange. It is an exchange between the status quo and a new possibility, between settling and stretching, certainty and wonderment, between death and life. It is watching someone who has never felt validated or good enough decide to finally stand and speak up, to take new action, to use his or her voice in a moment of transformation. It is a heroic act. It is that simple. It can be that simple. Sharing those moments creates something new in everyone present. It leaves a mark. We were designed to leave a mark—at some level—we all know this.

It is the deep and profound truth we wrestle with—it is what gets us out of bed in the morning or, alternatively, what keeps us in bed all day long. It is something C.S. Lewis called "the weight of glory." Every person, family, business, and community knows they can make a positive impact and leave a mark of beauty in this world. This frightening truth both dances with our insecurities and paints our dreams. The mark you leave is an impartation of your character on the heart of another person. Your 'marks' echo into eternity.

So, what do we do with this overwhelming reality? Most frequently, I would say, we resist it. It is frightening to think we are endowed with such power and beauty. And to face it—we must embrace the responsibility that comes with it. Resistance comes in many forms; procrastination, staying within the comfort zone of our known talents, cynicism, escapism (alcohol, drugs, Netflix, etc.) to name a few. Years ago, I read this quote and although I cannot quite remember where, it has stayed with me as a profound truth – and a gut punch.

"Some people are permanently angry or in a constant state of feeling sorry for themselves. The explanation? It's a common way

to avoid the anxiety of freedom, the fear of responsibility, the resistance against owning one's choices. The result? It keeps them infantilized forever, and none of the rewards of mature leadership will be available to them." – Peter Koestenbaum, author, philosopher, business consultant, and developer of the Leadership Diamond [1]

The "anxiety of freedom" blinds our eyes to what is forever present. We are the owners of our lives, our choices, and our impact on others. Again, we are made to mark one another.

How often do we allow our fears to drive us back into the smaller version of ourselves? Fear of failure, fear of what other people are thinking, fear of being exposed, fear of not being good enough, or smart enough—the list is endless. Much to our surprise, we find our great and glorious self does not quite fit stuffed into the cramped, tiny space that our fears allow. Our definitions of ourselves tend to be small so our leadership remains partially or completely dormant. If we are powerless to feed our own heroic selves, how will we feed and nurture the heroes in our midst?

Are you ready to feed the heroes around you by leading from the inside out?

The Proposition

First, consider that each moment, each engagement, every interaction is an opportunity for you to awaken your leadership, to allow it to come alive in a new way. You live your legacy in each moment. In the business world, it has often been called creating a WOW experience for your customer. It is powerfully imparting the values of the organization in an exchange with another person. Well, you are the CEO of YOU, right? You are in charge of what YOU do, of who you are and of the impact you make. Look at yourself as a business. What are your values? What is your WHY? What is your strategic plan? What are you passionate about, what truly makes you come alive—and how is that experience translated into your life with people? We are always making a mark or leaving an impression whether at work, at home, at the gym, or in the line at the coffee shop. We cannot help it. We are designed to do it. Even those days when internal resistance would have you believe otherwise, it is happening. Since you cannot stop it, you might as well steward it.

How do you find and then articulate a unique mark that is yours and yours alone to make? First, notice the internal conversation starting this very moment in your mind. Yes, right now. Are you saying to yourself, *it's already been done, I don't have anything to give, nothing is unique anymore, all I do is screw up*, or something along those lines?

If so, no problem. That is actually good news! It just means the resistance is alive and well in you. When that is happening, you know that there is something there to push against. In other words, resistance is a sign of life! In order to survive, you must have something to survive. So let's go again—what is the longing in your heart? What purpose lives in you to make manifest in the world? It can seem elusive and hard to define or so natural to us we may even miss when it is happening.

We are threatened daily, moment by moment, with the death of our dreams, the dulling of our purpose, the minimization of our gifting. These threats are not from any external force but from our own resistance. This resistance creates self-blindness, doubt, and compromise.

For years now I have resisted writing a book. I have had so many people ask me in the last eight years, "When are you writing a book?" Well, who said I was ever going to do that? I do not even keep a diary or journal regularly. Simply blogging on my website is a struggle most of the time. Yet, inwardly, I felt a draw to write this book. Whenever I felt that draw, I quickly pushed it back down, talked myself out of it, and resisted the calling. I did not want the discipline, was too busy, did not have anything to say. The truth is, I was afraid to be known.

Resistance is a wonderful thing—it is all around us and deeply rooted within us. I have noticed my own resistance morphs and takes on various forms. It runs from mild to wildly exaggerated. Sometimes it sounds like: *you don't have anything to say, you'll be judged for that, or no one cares.* Other times it is: *I'm stupid, I don't care, I don't make a difference, or no one likes me anyway.* You know the drill. What does yours sound like? Listen to the specific words in your head. What purpose are they serving? How long have you been giving them life, weight, and meaning? How many dreams have they killed? What opportunities have been missed? What relationships have died because you gave into that voice? The voice of resistance is an enemy to your legacy. It is like a blanket that seems to comfort but ultimately creates a cocoon that traps you in it threads. It will prod you, convince you, seduce you into really believing no one cares and nothing you have to offer is worthwhile. Worse, it tells you: *you are stupid, ridiculous, and something is probably wrong with you anyhow!*

I have had moments of resistance, days of resistance, weeks and even months of resistance. And I know you have too. No, I am not psychic, I am human. This is the human condition. We exist in the tension between what is and what could be, our comfort and our calling. It shows up in our personal lives, in our communities, and at our jobs. Whole organizations struggle to find the balance between creating value for their shareholders, delivering value to their customers, and being a place where their values are expressed daily in the lives of their employees. Giving in to the resistance slows the rate of motion in our lives. It puts life and relationships on repeat so we have the same experiences over and over. At long last, after about five or six years of pure, indulgent resistance, I sat down to write.

I started by telling many of my friends, "Hey I'm writing a book," mostly so I could not weasel out of it. Yes, I wanted their opinions and encouragement, but mostly I realized I needed to be provoked, to press on when the resistance whispered in my ear like a scorned lover, *Come back to me, it's so nice and comfortable here in the cocoon.*

Why am I starting a book about heroes, leadership, and legacy with resistance? Because giving in to resistance leads us to leave a certain type of legacy—not the kind I am interested in leaving. In your heroic journey, you are either moving in victory or in retreat. Resistance is a form of retreat. It is just part of life. It is in our DNA as human beings. It is possible, however, to notice the resistance and de-signify it. See it, feel it, and choose to go anyway—speak, act, or write. Just like a cat walking into the room, it is there, it may sit down and curl around your feet, but you do not have to give it all of your attention. Resistance does not have to be a formidable foe; it can be background noise or simply rocks in the path of your journey.

Take the time to identify the various ways your resistance shows up. There are obvious ways like *I don't want to get out of bed today* and subtler forms such as *I didn't have time.* Seriously, is there ever enough time?

Using time as a scapegoat for decision-making is one of the most popular forms of resistance. I have used it and seen it used frequently, especially when working with businesses. People and then whole departments get their identity from putting out fires, focusing on all the crises that seem to arise on a regular basis. When there is constant crisis and putting out of fires, it gives us convenient places to hide. We can amplify our version of being a savior, coming in and saving the day, by avoiding all the stuff we do not like to do or do not care to discipline ourselves to do. Some people make whole careers by doing it.

So when this is happening, what is not getting done? The regular everyday tasks, conversations, and processes. Why not? One reason is the daily tasks, the routines, require discipline and focus. Any type of discipline—whether physical, mental, emotional, relational—reveals our level of commitment and conversely our level of *entitlement.* We can see the results of discipline clearly in our lives. We get stronger, make more money, improve our skills, or develop our talents. Our entitlement, however, is harder to see. Even if it is obvious, we tend to explain it away, close our eyes, and not want to see it. Sometimes it is so subtle that we do not even recognize it as entitlement. At the end of the day, entitlement is the belief that *I should be able to have what I want when I want it.* When that does not happen, something is wrong—usually with someone or something else. Therefore, the risk is being revealed and exposed.

When we are exposed, others can see us. They can see our giftings, our flaws, and the roadblocks we throw up to avoid those giftings.

Start noticing the resistance in your life. It is not going anywhere so you might as well make friends with it.

"Most of us have two lives. The life we live, and the unlived life within us. Between the two stands Resistance....to yield to Resistance deforms our spirit. It stunts us and makes us less than we are and were born to be...it prevents us from achieving the life God intended when He endowed each of us with our own unique genius." –Steve Pressfield, author [2]

Sometimes we fool ourselves into thinking the life we are living is really all that is available. I know for me, at some fundamental level, it bothers me to be human. I think somehow that I should not have to be subject to faults, failure, or shortcomings. If I just worked hard enough, applied all my learning and resources, someday I would emerge as a being not encumbered by fear and insecurity or other strictly human emotions such as conceit and narcissism. To paraphrase William Glasser, renowned psychologist and author, in all of his decades of experience working with people, he noticed people have either one of two views of themselves: idealized or highly idealized.[3] In other words, highly flattering or pure fantasy. Yep, that is the spectrum. We are either extremely flattering in our hyperbole of ourselves—giving the benefit of the doubt, believing all of our intentions are good or conversely *I'm the worst person in the world.* (These are just two sides of the same coin.) Or we are in complete fantasy—unable to connect to, admit, or even see our dark side is with us all the time. We say things like *I know I'm not perfect.* Yet, we are intolerant of others who are not perfect. We cannot console ourselves for not being perfect yet hold imperfections against others.

"We confess our little faults to persuade people that we have no large ones." – Francois de La Rochefoucauld, author 4

This resistance to our own humanity steals valuable energy from our lives. Recognize that our flaws and shortcomings are just part of the operating system of a human being. I am not saying, "Hey, just resign yourself." Keep fighting and struggling with the natural tendency towards self-absorption. Just engage it as a constant part of life, not something that you will get over someday. Introduce yourself to it. Take it to dinner. Engage the heroic journey. Live a legacy now.

To be clear, let us define what I mean by the word hero. Heroism is the spirit with which you engage circumstance. Heroes are the ones who willingly enter into their own suffering as part of the journey. They are therefore unafraid to enter into the suffering of others. There is nothing superficial or shiny about the journey, it is about grit and love, the dirt and the glory. Heroes are not two-dimensional images of perfection. They are fully human, light and shadow, present here with an eye to the realm of the spirit, knowing any moment can be an opportunity to presence love, courage, and humility. It is getting up again and again without losing sight of why you started in the first place.

Leadership, including leading yourself, is the discipline and the privilege of calling out heroism. It involves feeding the aspects of our character that draw us towards vision with courage, care, and humility while being at peace with our imperfections. It is an art that requires a willingness to stand.

2

Being a Stand

When I got off the plane, the first thing I noticed was a billboard. *Welcome to Afghanistan, home of the brave.* Immediately I reflected back to countless baseball games and sporting events blasting the Star Spangled Banner and thought, *well I guess they can't really say land of the free and the home of the brave.* This was in June 2010. I entered a country that had been living in a state of conflict for over 30 years—needless to say, this was a new experience for me. I wondered about the people that I would meet—the lives about to intersect with mine on this new journey. I was nervous, excited, apprehensive, and absolutely compelled to meet the group of women that I had been distantly connected to for several months. I had the honor of contributing to the curriculum development for a women's leadership program piloted in Kabul. Now I was about to actually meet these women whom I had thought of, heard stories about, dreamed of, and prayed for over the past ten months.

I was conscious of my head cover, wanting to make sure it did not slip off. I worried if I was wearing it appropriately. Driving through the streets, through the round-a-bouts in the chaos of cars, mopeds, donkey carts, pedestrians, military personnel, and free-range animals was a full sensory experience. The land is dry, high desert. When we drove further into town, I noticed steel walls and gates, barbed wire, and the ruins of a war-torn city.

When I got to the office where I would be working, I only saw a building rising behind steel walls rimmed in barbed wire, a metal gate, and an eye slot in the gate to check visitors. As we were cleared to enter, the gate opened, and I saw five or six armed guards behind the gates on either side of our car as we drove in. Looking back, the fact that this became a normal occurrence is more jarring than the initial sight.

Inside, up the stairs in a large training room, were about forty women of all ages and professions. Some were young mothers, students, members of parliament, and some were women business owners. They had come from the city or from the outer provinces—sometimes traveling for a full day to reach their destination.

They had gathered together to learn—to learn about leadership, about their gifts, about what was possible in the face of so many limitations. When I stood up and introduced myself, I almost burst into tears. I felt so honored and so excited to be present with all these women. I could not wait to get started!

After the introductions, I asked them, "What does it mean to make a stand? To make a mark?" As I looked around the room, just a few women raised their hands. One woman, wearing a very conservative head covering, who seemed very quiet and reserved, slowly raised her hand. In my mind, I had already judged her as passive and compliant.

When I asked her to share, she said, "In my village, young girls were not allowed to be educated. This was wrong. I knew I needed to do something. So I decided to create a school in my home. The girls would come every day, hiding their schoolbooks in Quran covers to camouflage them. My next-door neighbor was Taliban but I didn't care. I did this for two years. I had to do it. Education is what will change our country."

I was simultaneously humbled by my own erroneous judgment and awed by her tremendous courage. This woman was living her legacy—NOW! She left a permanent mark on the lives of those girls; and in sharing her story, on my life and the lives of all the women in the room. She acted at great risk to herself. It was her purpose, her mark to leave in that moment. She may not have even fully comprehended what was imparted to each of those young girls. Did she struggle with resistance? I am sure she did. I can only imagine the fear and doubt that washed over her daily as she pushed through those conversations to open her doors once again, day after day. When I asked her what compelled her to do it, to take that risk, she simply replied, "It needed to be done." So many of the women there shared similar stories, I was inspired by their strength and courage, which they called "just doing what is needed."

The women I met were from all walks of life, all ages, from students to government officials. They shared their fears, concerns, victories, passions, and what mattered to them. We spoke of the ways they had been victimized, the ways they had participated in their own victimization, and what it means to open up a new future for their nation: to stand.

> *"We call them leaders because they go first."* – SIMON SINEK, AUTHOR, MOTIVATIONAL SPEAKER AND MARKETING CONSULTANT.[5]

I have had the privilege of working with leaders from around the globe. In each case, one of the first aspects I look for is the leader's willingness to make a stand—to take action. Making and/or being a stand is both an individual and a collective stance. It is a mood and an attitude, not a skill set or a personality style. It begins with a choice to take action and the choosing is never just about the individual, it is for the others impacted by the stand. It calls for perseverance—in the face of resistance (yours and others), lies, judgment, being undermined, and the constant invitation to settle. To be reduced to a lesser stance, to play games, give up, judge, and then hide.

A stand is a bold declaration FOR something, like the woman I met who stood to educate young girls in her village. It encompasses perseverance which presupposes suffering, things going wrong, things not being the way they should be. From a faith perspective, a stand is the cross; it is crucifying what you think it should look like, how people should be, all your insecurities and imagined failures and successes while not losing your footing. It is being anchored to the rock. It means the perceptual field is the eternal game, not the temporal one. When I am tempted to lash out, defend, or right half-truths and lies, instead, I stand.

How do you know if someone, or yourself, is being a stand? You will notice discomfort, perseverance, unprecedented faith and action, the creation of a sacred space for others to join and participate fully. It is not merely a good idea, those happen all the time; they come and go, usually engaged with some excitement that dies down when the circumstances push back. A stand rebuffs cynicism and invites vulnerability. When I think of a stand I recall a scene in *Forrest Gump* where Gary Sinise's character, the double-amputee Lieutenant Dan, hauls himself up the mast of the ship. He lashes himself near the top and cries out to God in the midst of the storm, "You call this a storm?!...It's time for a showdown!"[6]

A stand is evidenced by the way we engage our commitments and our relationships, the way we live out fellowship, partnership, and community. It creates an environment for learning, maturing, and thriving in the face of disappointment and loss. It is a way of being in community. It is the recognition that isolation leads to deception.

Who has made a stand in your life?

When you read that question, who comes to mind? Perhaps someone

you love or someone who loves you? Love itself demands a stand,
a re-ordering of priorities of personal comfort, of the overwhelming need
for certainty both in our circumstance as well as in others. Being a
stand involves a type of certainty that lies in who you are committed to
being in the midst of the chaos and uncertainty.

Ask yourself when others are dishonorable or disrespectful, do
you maintain your honor and respect? It is tempting to play down to the
level of whoever is lowering the bar, to create hurt when you are hurt,
perpetuating the pain. Love is a stand that creates space to absorb suffering
and remain steadfast. When love is elevated, fear and competition shrink.
Insecurities seem less and less significant and dissolve into the Great
Light. As the willingness to fully participate expands, new possibilities
open up. Beliefs cannot change without participation. The multiple times
Jesus spoke to repent, he was, in the vernacular, saying *change the way
you think.*

> *"Leadership has nothing to do with our title, position, tenure or
> 'span of control' and everything to do with the way we think."*
> –JOHN G. MILLER, AUTHOR OF FLIPPING THE SWITCH 7

When was the last time you changed your mind or recognized
a long-held belief was no longer working? What has been transformed in
your life? Maybe it is time to re-examine and explore what else may
be just as true or even truer. As you read, I invite you to stay curious.
If you look at the results in your life, what would they speak back to
you about your stand? When circumstances surprise you, what is your
automatic response?

3

Why Transformation?

Everyone in the room had tears in their eyes as the man spoke about his conversation with his neighbor. "I hadn't talked to him in ten years. We had a fight. I can't even remember what it was about. And I decided to cut him off. My family then stopped speaking to his family. When I went to him last night and told him I was done with our feud, we both wept. The truth was I have missed him. He was a friend. I allowed my pride to rob us of relationship for ten years. He felt the same way. Our relationship has been restored." It was 2011, in Kabul, Afghanistan. We were just starting Day 2 of a two-day Transformational Leadership training. Clearly, he had done his homework.

Many books, trainings, and seminars focus on learning new skill sets. And yes, skills are incredibly valuable and necessary. However, when new skills are added to an existing mindset, we often succeed in producing a slightly different version of what is already present. In this book, I am inviting you to transform your leadership. Not necessarily transform what you are doing, but the way of being or the attitude you automatically *presence*. Transformation involves a radical shift in how you see a person, a problem, a situation, a product, and most importantly—yourself. When I shift the way I see or relate to others, I can locate new possibilities for being with them. These transformations generate new action. Taking action is critical.

To take effective action first requires insight. Insight without action is simply mental assent to a concept. If I agree with an idea yet choose not to implement it, it is as if the idea never happened. This changes nothing yet allows the owner of the insight to tell themselves something has changed. As my dear friend, Hendre Coetzee, says, "Insight is the illusion of transformation. It feels great but nothing has really happened." Transformation requires movement.

Leadership is a way to capture the imagination and move people from their current state of reality towards vision; it is an invitation to their hero journey. It calls for a dynamic way of being and a willingness to continue learning, exploring, and most importantly—failing and getting up to go at it again. Making course corrections in real time is one of the hallmarks of a great leader.

In Daniel Coyle's book, *The Talent Code*, he illustrates how talent is actually built by attempting something, making a mistake, self-correcting, and going again.[8] Any transformation requires this type of discipline— making friends with what other people call 'failure.' Embrace the fail! The fail is what makes the victory possible.

> *"The key to transformation is time, intensity, and repetition."*
> –Dallas Willard, American philosopher [9]

In our *three strikes you're out* culture, we have lost the value of perseverance. The repetition part of the formula is undermined by our aversion to failure. The culture informs us if something feels bad then it is bad and to be avoided. We have this idea that if you are learning something new, you should be able to do that something well the first time you do it. When that fantasy evaporates, the default reactions are to blame or walk away. So often when working with leaders around the world I hear them say, "Oh, I tried that, it doesn't work." Really? How many times did you try it? If it is a conversation with someone, it may necessitate more than one shot (or twenty, depending on the value of the relationship). The risk of going, again and again, involves the possibility of repeated failure, rejection, or disappointment. Any leader who resists this reality will remain in their proverbial comfort zone and will become, well, comfortable—and ultimately irrelevant.

Transformation involves risk. In many ways, it is a violent process. It violates our comfort, our view of ourselves, our view of others, our view of our circumstance and ultimately, our relationship to God. It is a risk to release what is known and reach for what is unknown and unprecedented. Transformational leaders are willing to make the exchange time and time again.

> *"To be great, struggle is not an option, it's a biological requirement."* – DANIEL COYLE, AUTHOR [10]

Think of it like this: incremental change or growth is measuring movement based on what has been, on your past history, or experience. It is characterized by the use of language such as more, better, or different. Consider the statement *I want to be a better leader.* Better is a relative term, it is past-based. Better than what? If you are a terrible leader right now, better is not going to get you to great. You could simply advance from terrible to bad. From this viewpoint, we can only expect incremental movement and certainly nothing unprecedented.

In a transformative mindset, significant leaps are possible. Transformation is not based on your history or your past or even your experience. It is based on a new way of thinking and being; a declaration followed up by committed action. One of the underlying assumptions here is we have the ability to be whoever we choose in any given moment.

Perhaps you are familiar with the old Cherokee tale of the two wolves. An old Cherokee chief was teaching his grandson about life:

"A fight is going on inside me," he said to the boy. "It is a terrible fight and it is between two wolves. One is evil - he is anger, envy, sorrow, regret, greed, arrogance, self-pity, guilt, resentment, inferiority, lies, false pride, superiority, self-doubt, and ego. The other is good - he is joy, peace, love, hope, serenity, humility, kindness, benevolence, empathy, generosity, truth, compassion, and faith. This same fight is going on inside you - and inside every other person, too."
The grandson thought about it for a minute and then asked his grandfather, "Which wolf will win?"
The old chief simply replied, "The one you feed."

In 2015, I was in South Africa, Cape Flats, working with a sixth-grade class at Perivale School. Cape Flats is one of the most underserved, violent, gang-infested areas in South Africa. The sixth graders live with their parents and relatives being shot, stabbed, imprisoned, or drug addicted. There are regular shoot-outs on the streets. After-school programs are non-existent because it is unsafe to walk home after 3 or 4 in the afternoon. My nonprofit, GAP Community, has had the privilege of serving in South Africa since 2006.

Standing in front of the class after spending two days of training on vision, value, and voice, I was struggling to find a way to communicate clearly to these kids the value of choice. I recalled the old Cherokee tale and reworked it a bit. I asked, "Do you think you have a hero inside of you?" A few answered with no, some with maybe and then silence. I reminded them Nelson Mandela grew up not far from this school. Was he a hero?

"Yes!"

"Can you make the same kind of choices he made?" A few yeses, but mostly still hesitation.

New question. "Ok, do you think you have a criminal inside of you?" A loud yes! came back to me. "So let's say you have both, a hero and a criminal inside, and they're fighting. Who is going to win?"

"The strongest one!" they say.

"Yes! And how do you get strong?"

"You build your muscles and eat food!"

"Perfect," I say. "So what choices feed your hero?" We made a list on the board, I heard: "be nice to my sister," "tell the truth," "don't steal," and more. Then I asked, "What choices feed your criminal?"

I heard: "being mean," "taking what's not yours," "lying to people," and more. It created a great context for them to consider their choices and where their choices were taking them.

And it is not just for kids! As a leader, one of my primary responsibilities is to call forth the hero in the people I serve. If you listen closely to people's conversation you can hear when they put their cape on, when their purpose comes alive, passion gets sparked, and they are playing all in. Listen for those moments; feed those moments as a leader. And no, not everyone will take you up on your invitation. It is ok. Work with those who are willing. As the saying goes, you can't push a rope.

Even though I know not everyone is willing, I choose to assume people want to be heroic. I operate from that assumption because it changes me and the way I relate to the people I meet. When I go in thinking *not everybody will want this* I notice I immediately start separating people in my mind between those who do and those who do not. And I am often wrong. I decided if I was going to be wrong, I would rather be wrong by thinking the best and being disappointed instead of assuming someone was not interested and not giving 100% to have it happen. I know transformation is always possible.

4

What is Transformation?

"And do not be conformed to this world, but be transformed by the renewing of your mind..." –St. Paul [11]

How do we renew our minds? We must start by examining our thoughts, especially the ones we do not say aloud. As you read, allow yourself to think about your thinking. It can be challenging to think about your thinking, especially since you are the one thinking! Start by noticing your thoughts instead of just being immersed in them, as if they are all true. All of our thoughts make sense to us; thoughts seem correct in our mind. However, only when we put those thoughts out into the light can they be examined and sifted. Our natural tendency is to polarize our thoughts into good/bad, right/wrong, and honor/shame.

Since most of us do not want to be associated with anything bad, wrong, or shameful, we do not often own these thoughts long enough to explore them or as I like to say, *wonder into them.* If we do not want to see certain thoughts, we will not be able to examine them. Whatever is unexamined has no chance of being renewed. So we tend to live in an unexamined state around our shadow side.

Our shadow side houses the thoughts, beliefs, and feelings we would rather not see in ourselves. When they surface, we push them quickly away with a platitude or a rationalization. It might sound something like, *oh I'm not really upset that someone got credit for my work or that I didn't receive recognition for something. I'm just glad they were acknowledged.* While there might be some truth in this statement, it simply may not be the full truth. It is laced with an undercurrent of should—as in, I should not feel this way or think this, so I will not.

As a human being, I am a living paradox. I am temporal and eternal, body and spirit, light and dark, dust and glory. Transformation is only possible when we are willing to embrace this reality. The fantasy of perfectionism only invites despair.

Remember William Glasser's assertion? People have one of two views of themselves: either highly flattering or pure fantasy. I will admit when I first read this, I was slightly offended. I thought, *who does he think he is?!* However, since I am in the business of asking people to try on new ideas, I decided to try it on. When I say *try it on* what I mean is I assume it is true. I do this long enough to see where, when, and how it may be true. So I used Glasser's assertion as a vantage point to examine my life, my thoughts, my habits, and my conversations. I began to notice I have specific conversations about the way I am. I am this kind of person, not that kind of person.

For example, I see myself as responsible. This view necessarily blinds me to the areas and relationships where I behave irresponsibly. And if someone brings it to my attention, my first response is to defend or explain. I think, *you don't understand* or *you don't know me.* In this way, I refuse to examine or renew my mind in that one area. I do not like what is being revealed, my flattering self-view rejects it. *Voilà!* A blind spot.

As a leader, we naturally pass our blind spots down throughout our organization. Ronald Heifetz, Senior Lecturer in Public Leadership at

Harvard's John F. Kennedy School of Government, suggests, "Mastering the courage to interrogate reality is a central function of a leader."[12] Current reality includes hard data as well as what is going on subjectively for each person in the organization, including the leader. Often we swing one way or the other, rarely taking stock in the value of the entire context of the people we are with by exploring their thoughts and feelings as well as the results.

Examining current reality requires both courage and humility: the courage to look and the humility to own when our thoughts and habits are out of alignment with what we say we want and who we say we are. Ancient writers remind us of God's word to the prophet Isaiah:

"For My thoughts are not your thoughts,
Nor are your ways My ways," says the Lord.

"For as the heavens are higher than the earth,
So are My ways higher than your ways,
And My thoughts than your thoughts."[13]

If we keep in mind the reality that our thoughts are not the same as God's thoughts, it is easier to remain open to both hearing new thoughts as well as examining our own. In other words, we never have the full picture. We see only part of what is present.

We naturally default to our own control, devices, strategies, and protection. This is our survival nature; it is part of our DNA. It has been with us since the beginning of time so it is probably not going away. What we do with it is our choice. It is part of our current reality.

Remember, current reality includes all the results, the hard data, the emotional context, the culture, other people and their perspectives and ideas, our experiences—everything that makes up our reality. (I know; it would be easier if it did not include those other people!)

One trap leaders fall into is failing to take into account the reality of those around them. If we are only looking at our part of reality, we miss a huge chunk of what is actually present. While we may not agree with others' version of reality, it still affects the way we work and/or live together.

As we interrogate the full version of reality, we discover resources to be utilized in pursuit of our vision: resources in the form of what is working, what is not working, blind spots, patterns, and incongruities. Ignoring or avoiding current reality frustrates our pursuit of vision. Whenever we feel thwarted or frustrated on the journey towards our vision, unsure of what to do next, it can be traced back to feedback or data we are missing in our current reality.

Moment by moment, we can choose to surrender to our current reality or to resist it and live the fantasy of how life should or should not be. It is impossible to explore what you resist. Surrendering is not the same as giving up, resigning, or despairing. On the contrary, surrendering in this context allows you to be present with what is there and who is there and choose from that space. Giving up says *I don't want to continue;* resigning says *it doesn't matter anyway;* and despairing says *it's never going to be any different.* Surrender says *I see what's happening and receive it as reality. Now I can make a new choice based on what is.* Surrender allows you to persevere, care, and hold onto hope with courage and commitment.

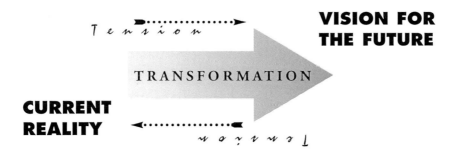

Consider the vision you have for your life, your family, or your organization. It exists in the future; the future you see as possible. However, we do not live in the future, we live in the present and are steeped in the current reality of our lives. Notice the diagram shows two arrows labeled "tension."

There are two kinds of tension; one is the tension drawing us up towards our vision. It is the longing, the draw, and the purpose compelling us to get out of bed in the morning and move towards our vision, to take the next step. The other is the tension to lower our vision to the level of our current reality. It is the conversation that sounds like *did I say that was my vision? That's too big, I don't know what I was thinking. This is fine.* It is the voice encouraging us to play a small game, one we can predict and control. If what you call your vision is within your ability to manage or control, if it does not require risk, faith, or surrender, then it is probably just a good idea.

Vision is necessarily beyond our reach, it calls for us to collaborate with God and step beyond our comfort, ability, and/or strategies. The discipline to explore current reality is necessary to effectively pursue vision.

I was working with a local church that had received a resignation notice from their worship leader. We were in a staff meeting and had just informed the rest of the staff about the change. The worship leader and their spouse shared their heart and said that God was moving them into something new, even though the path was not clear yet. After a few minutes of sharing and some questions, the senior pastor said, "Okay, let's go ahead and pray for them right now!"

I jumped in, saying, "Yes, we will pray for them but not yet. Let's keep exploring." I used a set of questions to slow down the process and investigate the current reality for the team.

1. What did you hear?

I wanted to check in and see if what people were hearing was what was actually being said. Also, it is important to align the team and make sure no one is missing data. Then I asked the next question.

2. What do you feel about this change?

This is a critical step. I used an easel pad to capture everyone's feelings. There were many: sad, excited, confused, disappointed, anxious, etc. People began sharing their hearts for this couple and also began self-reflecting on their own lives. If we ignored this emotional context of our team, we would miss valuable information for calibrating current reality. Emotion drives decision. While working with brain-damaged patients, neuroscientist Antonio Damasio discovered people with damage to the emotional centers of their brains were unable to make good decisions. His work revealed all choice is initiated from an emotional context. People make decisions emotionally first and then back those decisions up with rational thinking.

3. What are you making it mean or how are you filling in the blanks?

People naturally fill in the rest of the story for whatever data is missing. The mind cannot tolerate an open loop. Lithuanian psychologist Bluma Zeigarnik discovered this principle in 1927 while noticing how waiters

remembered tabs at a local restaurant. Waiters remembered incomplete tabs
more clearly than they remembered complete ones. In future studies by
Zeigarnik and other psychologists since, we have learned the mind is more
likely to remember incompletions and keep cycling through them.[14]
(More on this later, it can work in our favor as leaders!) Since our survival
mechanism is always working to conserve energy, we often fill in blanks
for data we do not have to stop the cycling. The staff had filled in the blanks
with: "they're probably leaving the church," "they are in breakdown with
the leadership," "they disagree with the way we are doing things here," etc...
While there may be some truth in any of these assumptions, it is impossible to
test it out if the conversations remain hidden or unexamined. Getting these
conversations out into the light was integral to moving forward.

After we moved through these three questions (it took about forty
minutes, in case you are worried this process takes too long), we prayed.
It was relevant and deeply intimate. I am not suggesting you use this
process for every decision. However, I recommend it for navigating change
with your team. Change is often thought of as an incremental process.
Transformation allows you and your teams to make tremendous leaps in
productivity, connectedness, and efficiency.

To begin our journey of transformation, the renewing of our minds,
we first must notice the way we are currently thinking. The Old
Testament prophet, Jeremiah, says it this way:

> *"Let us examine our ways and test them and let us return*
> *to the Lord."* [15]

Examining our ways means to search out the journey of our life, the
habits and patterns we live in, the conversations we automatically engage
about God, others, and ourselves. Testing our ways involves trying
them out, measuring them against our vision, paying attention to the
results we have in every area of our lives. Notice the last part of this verse

"…and let us return to the Lord." Here is an assumptive statement—if we diligently examine and test our ways, we will see how we have departed from the Lord. If you have difficulty connecting with the term 'Lord' then you can substitute whatever you use as the plumb line for your attitude of heart and behavior in life.

We will see how we have taken our own path, believed our own press, indulged our self-flattering or fantastical views of ourselves and we will be humbled. In our humility, we have the opportunity to return, to repent, to change our minds, to re-engage our relationships. Without self-awareness and a willingness to shift what we see, this type of realignment is not available.

> *"Although it is probably one of the least discussed leadership competencies, self-awareness is possibly one of the most valuable. Self-awareness is being conscious of what you're good at while acknowledging what you still have yet to learn. This includes admitting when you don't have the answer and owning up to mistakes.*
>
> *In our highly competitive culture, this can seem counterintuitive. In fact, many of us operate on the belief that we must appear as though we know everything all the time or else people will question our abilities, diminishing our effectiveness as leaders. If you're honest with yourself, you'll admit that really the opposite is true. Because whether you acknowledge your weaknesses or not, everyone still sees them. So rather than conceal them, the person who tries to hide weaknesses actually highlights them, creating the perception of a lack of integrity and self-awareness."*
> – Inc. Magazine – October 2007, Chris Musselwhite [16]

Musselwhite makes a compelling point here. As a leader, our power and influence are tied to our humility. The term servant leader is overused but the point is well taken. Without humility, we are naturally tempted to serve ourselves, to elevate our agenda, and feed the monster of our fantasy view of ourselves, as William Glasser discovered. When our WHY (our dominant driving purpose) is simply servicing our self-view, our leadership suffers because those around us become tools instead of people capable of greatness, care, and connection.

In chapters 8 through 13, we are going to explore six distinctions around leadership. As we review each one, I invite you to try them on like a new jacket. Take off whatever you currently believe about yourself and put on the distinction as if it is the first time you have ever considered it. Look at your life and all of your relationships from the vantage point of each distinction and see what opens up. Instead of looking for what you already know or do, be curious about where else you can engage and presence these distinctions whether at home, at work, or in your community. While these are not intended to be the only characteristics of a leader, they are the ones we will be considering throughout. If the inquiry is going to be valuable, it is going to change who you are instead of just giving you an answer. Soren Kierkegaard, a brilliant 19th Century philosopher, theologian, and social critic wrote, "Seek the truth so that the process of the inquiry transforms the seeker to a place where the object of the pursuit may reside."[17] It is a call to transcend your sense of self and fully engage in what it takes to presence leadership. It requires a willingness to challenge our existing ways of thinking and paradigms.

> *CURRENT REALITY CHECK: Is your vision big enough to call you into uncharted waters or is it something you can handle by yourself? When you examine your ways, what do you notice? How aware are you of your own emotional context and the emotional context of your team?*

5

Paradigms

Paradigm is simply another way of saying worldview or belief systems. Paradigm is defined as a fundamental, unquestioned set of assumptions that determine our worldview. Since paradigms are unquestioned, we live at the mercy of their presumed accuracy, creating blind spots in our perceptive field. These blind spots remain until we are willing to engage the possibility that we do not know what we think we know. Since we are hard-wired to be right, it can certainly be destabilizing to begin the inquiry. Being curious, living in wonderment instead of certainty, allows new information to penetrate our natural self-protection. Beliefs shift as they are questioned and explored. Check out this advertisement from the late 1880s:

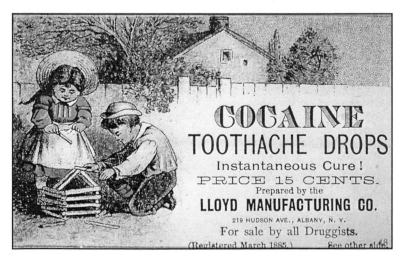

COCAINE
TOOTHACHE DROPS
Instantaneous Cure!
PRICE 15 CENTS.
Prepared by the
LLOYD MANUFACTURING CO.
219 HUDSON AVE., ALBANY, N. Y.
For sale by all Druggists.
(Registered March 1885.)   See other side.

Or this one from the 1900s:

At the point in time these advertisements were made, this was popular pseudoscience. It was customary. People were making the best choice they saw possible with the data they had at the time. In 2018, chances are most people would not give their infants cocaine drops to stave off teething pain. Nor would most people recommend a soft drink before dinner to curb the appetite given what we have now learned about the health risks of consuming soft drinks and sugar in general. There are countless examples ranging from the benefits of smoking cigarettes to recommending wine for depression.

Each one of us can think back to a belief we held years ago that now may seem absurd or at the very least, immature. It is part of being human. Look at some of the beliefs you hold around leadership. Who is a leader? What does a leader look like? What would make a good or a bad leader in your opinion? Be willing to explore and inquire into whatever beliefs and experiences you have in order to continue learning and expand your perceptual field.

As learning continues to expand our horizons, we are able to try on new lenses to view our world. Here are another few examples from a history of paradigm blindness.

"The phonograph... is not of any commercial value."

   - THOMAS EDISON 1880 [18]

"Flight by machines heavier than air is unpractical and insignificant, if not utterly impossible."

   - SIMON NEWCOMB - ASTRONOMER 1902 [19]

"It is an idle dream to imagine that.....Automobiles will take the place of railways in the long-distance movement of passengers."

   - AMERICAN ROAD CONGRESS 1913 [20]

"Who wants to hear actors talk?"

   - HARRY WARNER, WARNER BROTHERS PICTURES 1927 [21]

"I think there is a world market for about five computers."

   - THOMAS J. WATSON, CHAIRMAN OF IBM, 1943 [22]

Every one of these examples was spoken by people who were experts in their field. They were on the cutting edge of current knowledge and understanding. Yet what they knew as possible also determined what was not possible. Once I decide something is not possible, I will naturally stop challenging or questioning it. It would seem like a waste of time or energy. Often individuals from other disciplines or with less experience provoke learning as they more easily question existing assumptions. In Frans Johannson's book *The Medici Effect*, Johannson examines the benefit of combining people from various cultures, crafts, and expertise to birth extraordinary new ideas.[23] It is remarkable how the intersections of these varied perspectives and ways of thinking solve existing problems and innovate new methodology, products, and structures in the fields of architecture, science, business, and medicine. What could a new perspective from a completely different field do for you or your business?

> *"If you wear glasses, you likely often forget that they're even there! Only when you take the lenses off do you realize how much your capacity to see is informed by the lens through which you are seeing."* – Cynthia Bourgeault Ph.D., Episcopal priest, teacher and author [24]

While paradigm is a painfully overused word, it still captures the concept of mindset plus perception. Thomas Kuhn, a physicist, historian, and philosopher, coined the term paradigm shift in 1962. For him, a paradigm shift meant a cataclysmic change; a revolutionary breakthrough into something new. His work opened doors for new ways of thinking and being in the realm of science and historical analysis. Kuhn created a philosophy of science, acting as a platform for learning and inquiry. [25]

> *"Paradigms act as physiological filters - that we quite literally see the world through our paradigms ... Data that exists in the real world that does not fit your paradigm will have a difficult time getting through your filters… What we actually perceive is dramatically determined by our paradigms. What may be perfectly visible, perfectly obvious to persons with one paradigm, may be, quite literally invisible to persons with a different paradigm. This is the paradigm effect."* – Joel Arthur Barker, technology and business futurist and author [26]

This is really quite remarkable. A physiological barrier (did you read psychological?) is body and mind. Neuroscience has discovered there is no distinction between the body and the mind; they operate in tandem, as one. The mind is a direct result of physiology. Therefore, paradigms prevent us from actually seeing with our eyes what may be right in front of us.

Because our brain is already adept at editing, generalizing, deleting, and distorting information, paradigms simply apply additional filters to this naturally occurring process. Before you attempt to find and destroy your filters, stop. It is not possible and they are necessary.

Dr. Joseph Dispenza, DC writes: "The human body sends 400 billion bits of information per second to the brain for processing, yet the conscious mind is only aware of 2,000 of those."[27] Therefore, we must filter. We are designed to filter. It is part of how we survive. So do not worry! Did you immediately think of filters as bad or something to eradicate? Instead of wondering *how can I get rid of my filters?* Perhaps wonder instead *what I am filtering in this moment?* Or wonder *what else can be just as true as what I've already decided?*

I invite you to take on a beginner's mind—to remain open—as you work through this process. What you currently know is great and valuable, but it can also constrain your new learning. I am not asking you to give up what you know; I am inviting you to give up your *attachment* to it—to hold it lightly. Remember, the way you hold what you know influences your attitude. Attitude is the environment of your being, your leadership, and your presence.

Take a minute and do a short exercise. On a piece of paper or on your computer or phone, begin a sentence with "women are" then write as many adjectives as immediately come to mind. No editing or taking time to think it through (or be politically correct), just whatever first pops into your head. Next, use "men are" and do the same exercise. Then you can add any ethnicity, type of driver, religion, or opposing political party member and do the same exercise. Give yourself fully to the process, remember … no editing or attempting to get the right answer. This is just for you.

Now stop. Notice what you see. Do you imagine everyone reading this book completed the sentences in the same way? Of course not. Also, notice if you resisted the exercise.

Now whether you would say you really think this way or not, notice how automatically the adjectives occurred. All of these beliefs came from somewhere, whether you would say they are accurate or not, fair or not, realistic or not. They live internally as paradigms, filters, or assumptions. To have a new experience of someone in any of these areas, we must release or at least hold lightly what we already expect or imagine.

We See What We Expect to See:

You are quite literally unable to
to perceive data before your very eyes

Did you catch a mistake? If not, keep looking.

The willingness to explore and examine the underlying assumptions around God, others, and myself is at the core of effective leadership. As mentioned earlier in the book, one of the primary functions of a leader is to have the courage to interrogate reality. Not just external reality but also the version living in our heads.

So how to do we begin the journey? Like any other adventure, we begin with a commitment to fully engage and remain present to whatever comes our way.

> *"Until one is committed there is hesitancy, the chance to draw back, always ineffectiveness. Concerning all acts of initiative (and creation), there is one elementary truth, the ignorance of which kills countless ideas and splendid plans: that the moment one definitely commits oneself-then Providence moves too. All sorts of things occur to help one that would never otherwise have occurred. A whole stream of events issues from the decision raising in one's favor all manner of unforeseen incidents and meetings and material assistance, which no man could have dreamt could have come his way."* - W. H. MURRAY, EXPLORER [28]

You may recognize the names as one of the explorers who conquered Mount Everest. If you have ever seen the IMAX movie or read any accounts of what it is like to scale Everest, you already know it is not just daunting but also incredibly dangerous. Yet somehow, this type of relentless commitment opens the door to resourcefulness, locating resources in the midst of any circumstance.

It was 2010 in Kabul, Afghanistan. Two young women, ages sixteen and seventeen, decided to do their final leadership project by offering to teach a two-hour session on what they were learning in One Voice, a twelve-month women's leadership development program I co-authored. They went to the women in their village knocking on doors and inviting them to come and participate. The village women were not interested, did not believe they could learn from such young women and closed their doors to the invitation. The two students came back to class discouraged by the results. Their coach reminded them of their commitment. So the two women went back to their village to go again.

When they returned, they noticed the men of the village met in a certain spot every week so they decided to go and invite them (this is culturally unheard of). The men laughed at their invitation and continued their meeting. The two students thought *if we go back, our coach is going to ask us, 'what's another possibility?' so we might as well think of one and move forward.* They decided to go back to the men's meeting and persist with their request. Eventually, one of the men said, "Okay, you can have an hour." The students were elated … nervous, but elated. They stood up and began training on what they had been learning about leadership. At first, the men scoffed and made disrespectful comments. Nevertheless, these two brave young women persisted. After a short time, the men began listening. At the end of their time, the leader in the men's meeting told these young women he had learned something and asked them to come back. Unprecedented! When the young women returned, they found the women of the village, who had snubbed the initial invitation, also sitting in the room. Side note: the program was designed for women eighteen and over but these two made it through the interview phase somehow without being asked their age!

Edwin Friedman in his book *A Failure of Nerve* describes leadership as "maintaining a non-anxious, well-principled presence in the midst of a reactive and chronically anxious society or group."[29] These two young women stayed the course, took action, and were not swayed by the reactivity and anxiety of the village.

Whenever I become discouraged or daunted by my circumstances, I recall the bravery and resilience of these young women. They not only taught the men and women of the village valuable lessons in leadership but they *presenced* the spirit of leadership in a way that inspires me to this day. Ask yourself, what is your capacity for *presence*? It is intimately connected to your attitude and your willingness to move forward in the face of perceived obstacles. Some call it grit. St. Paul puts it this way:

> *"…we also glory in our sufferings, because we know that suffering produces perseverance; perseverance, character; and character, hope. And hope does not put us to shame"* [30]

The willingness to press on, to stand, is a continual choice. Commit to learning, to identifying and challenging your assumptions and to practice relentless curiosity, especially in the arenas or relationships you think of as the most familiar. It is an exercise in courage and humility. Hero food.

> *CURRENT REALITY CHECK: Did you take the time to do the exercises in this chapter or did you blow past them because you already know? How often have you been surprised by changes in the marketplace, the competition, customers' or family's needs? Where can you identify your knowing as a hindrance to your learning? What suffering or obstacles have you persevered in and when have you given up?*

6

Who is Driving the Train?

"You can't change a person's performance until you first change their beliefs." –Francis Frei, Senior Associate Dean, Harvard Business School [31]

Consider this model of behavior: it starts with our internal conversations, which reveal our unconscious, even in our pre-verbal state, based on our environment and familial relationships. These continue to form and shift throughout our lives. All of our experiences, our culture, our religion, our education, our family background etc... build and fortify our belief systems.

Our beliefs generate our emotions or feelings. In addition, our feelings are the fuel for our actions, behavior, and words. All of our beliefs create a filter for the way we see reality. We are constantly, and mostly unconsciously, looking at the world around us through a filter designed to validate our existing beliefs about God, others, and ourselves.

Let us look at an example. If I have the belief *I can't trust my team*, what will be the effect? Well, for one thing, I will be suspicious and guarded around them. I will naturally be looking for proof that I am right. I will seek evidence to support my assumptions. Perhaps I will find myself being nervous, suspicious, self-protective, or defensive when we are together. I may double check their work or resist delegation.

Maybe I allow cynicism to color my speech and my listening during our meetings. In doing so, I create a certain type of environment or culture. I shut off anything that is not what I want to see. This is called observer bias in psychology. We have a bias towards something and we focus on validating our bias and ignore other data which is also present. Sometimes we even see things that are not really there—simply because we are looking so hard.

Have you ever been around someone who was suspicious of you? Had someone watch your every move or continually question your motives? How would you describe that experience? After a short time, it is natural to withdraw and protect yourself in response. You may think, *it's not safe to share honestly, I'm already defeated before I begin*, or *I better have everything right before I present my idea*, or even *I need to fix this mistake quickly before they find out*. All kinds of internal conversations and emotions are generated which in turn create an almost self-fulfilling prophecy.

As a leader, if I have this belief, what type of people will I naturally hire? The ones who cannot be trusted. Why? My radar is automatically tuned to them! Even if I manage to hire someone who is trustworthy, the culture will often wear him or her down over time. So that three months or six months from now, when a team member lies, withholds information, or covers up a mistake, I can say, "See I was right! I can't trust them!" And why? So I can get rid of that one and go find another one I cannot trust? Because, at the end of the day, I would rather be right about my belief than trust and risk disappointment or allow some-one else to do the important work in my organization.

Our beliefs are so strong, we would rather be right than have our relationships work out, or be fulfilled in our families, careers, or to live healthy lives. Yes, the reality is we would rather be right than be fulfilled.

It is a hard truth to consider. Notice if you are already rejecting it before you consider where or when it may be true. Recall Glasser's quote on our view of ourselves ranging from highly flattering to pure fantasy. This is a common place for fantasy to live, denying my underlying need to be right at all costs.

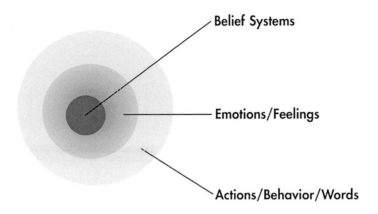

Belief Systems

Emotions/Feelings

Actions/Behavior/Words

Since most of us are not crazy, we do what we do for reasons, reasons that align with our beliefs. We get goodies or payoffs for every action we choose - even the ones we would say cause harm, chaos, or sabotage in our lives.

Look at the conversation around trust. If I am living in a conversation that says *I can't trust my team*, I am getting something out of it. I am also paying prices for it.

PAYOFFS	PRICES
Being right	Loneliness
Safety	Isolation
Staying comfortable	Judgment
Avoiding risk	Missing data in current reality
Being in control	Frustration
Looking good to others and myself	Stagnation
	Anger
Being superior	Sadness
	Expense by continually having to retrain new people
	Pressure
	Disappointment
	Lies

Take any result you have and break it down for yourself. Be honest and do some forensics on your choices. The payoffs are always personal, just for you. They are things we do not typically like to admit. Unfortunately, they are not very flattering after all.

The prices are paid not only by you but also by those around you. Test it. You will find there are plenty of conversations lurking in your blind spots waiting to be uncovered.

Another way to describe this dynamic is the psychological concept of cognitive dissonance. *Psychology Today* writes: "If you've ever told a lie and felt uncomfortable because you see yourself as scrupulously honest, then you've experienced cognitive dissonance. It occurs when your ideas, beliefs, or behaviors contradict each other: if, for example, you see yourself as smart but cannot believe you made such dumb stock investments. Exactly how we choose to resolve the dissonance (and its accompanying discomfort) is a good reflection of our mental health. In fact, cognitive dissonance can be a great opportunity for growth." [32]

We have all had conflicting beliefs. It is part of being human. One conversation says, *Get up and go for a run!* The competing conversation says, *Stay in bed; it's so comfy here!* St. Paul expressed it this way in his letter to the Romans:

"I do not understand what I do. For what I want to do I do not do, but what I hate I do. And if I do what I do not want to do, I agree that the law is good. As it is, it is no longer I myself who do it, but it is sin living in me. I know that nothing good lives in me, that is, in my sinful nature. For I have the desire to do what is good, but I cannot carry it out. For what I do is not the good, I want to do; no, the evil I do not want to do—this I keep on doing. Now if I do what I do not want to do, it is no longer I who do it, but it is sin living in me that does it. So I find this law at work: When to do good, evil is right there with me. For in my inner being I delight in God's law; but I see another law at work in the members of my body, waging war against the law of my mind and making me a prisoner of the law of sin at work within my members." [33]

You may be familiar with Sigmund Freud's iceberg theory. Here is an illustration:

In nature, only about 10% of an iceberg is above the surface of the water. The bulk of it is hidden underneath.[34] Freud posits we are only aware or conscious of about 10% of our motivations and beliefs. The rest live beneath the surface. While we may never fully be able to explore our entire iceberg, there are ways we can lower the water line.

When we experience cognitive dissonance in our leadership, it is a wonderful opportunity to learn something about ourselves and engage the discipline which character development requires. It provides both a humbling and revelatory moment where the truth does indeed set us free—right after it violates our flattering view of ourselves!

CURRENT REALITY CHECK: What was illuminated for you? Create your own personal payoffs & prices chart. What do you notice? What conflicting intentions have you experienced in your leadership lately?

7

Characteristics of a Leader

Learner

Ears to Hear

Adaptable

Direction

Environment

Responsibility and results

For the next six chapters, we will be exploring each characteristic. I recommend you apply them to yourself first and then consider your team or those you lead. The November-December 2017 issue of *Harvard Business Review* cites, "Organizations around the world are failing on one key metric of success: leadership development." The success rates for leadership development programs have dropped in the past three years from a low 17% to a lower 13%. Instead of just measuring competencies, they have started to link specific competencies to four traits which strengthen them: curiosity, insight, engagement, and determination.[35] It is clear leadership development is a critical component in any industry, organization, or family. In the next six chapters, you will see how these traits play into the characteristics listed above. You will have insight into practical application of these principles.

As we dissect each characteristic, ask yourself *how often do I model this one?* You may find some come more naturally than others may. Allow each one to be a platform for you, a lens to view your everyday leadership. Each one is a discipline, something requiring regular practice.

Notice if you have already gotten distracted by what you think is missing from this list. Relax. It is not intended to be a comprehensive list of every possible characteristic. These are just the ones we will be exploring in this book.

In a recent study on leadership completed by Harvard University validating the Harrison assessment tool, researchers linked effective leadership to the ability to maintain flexibility in paradox. For example, there is a natural tension between candor and diplomacy. Neither end of the spectrum is always the right call. Leaders who pay attention to context develop the ability to discern when to use which skill set. As you practice modeling the distinctions listed, you will notice an increased awareness and ability to expand your way of being beyond your natural default.

Your natural default is not good or bad, it is simply resourceful in some contexts but not in every context. The ability to position yourself to read the situation and the people involved as if it is new each time is a discipline which requires curiosity, which produces insight, which leads to engagement. Determination is the commitment to persevere in the transformation as it unfolds, usually messy and full of surprises along the way. Consider it your own personal heroic adventure!

8

The Leader as a Learner

"It is impossible for a man to begin to learn what he thinks he knows." – Epictetus, philosopher [36]

Leaders are perpetual learners. They adopt a learning stance in life and are willing to challenge the status quo, their own assumptions, and winning strategies while recognizing that their view is always limited, never complete.

Too often we are driven by our egos—our personal need to be right or to prove something. While we do have plenty of knowledge and expertise since most of us are paid to be experts in our fields—sometimes we fall short. What I am addressing here is not your knowledge, it is the attitude of heart you have towards what you know. How do you hold it? Tightly? Loosely? With defense? With curiosity? If we can maintain a learning stance, a beginner's mind in the midst of our knowledge, we will be able to effectively calibrate current reality. A learning stance allows us to hear feedback effectively, consider it, and apply it without unnecessary resistance. Whenever I am stuck defending what I already know, it is a red flag that I have closed my mind to learning.

"Now we see only a reflection as in a mirror; then we shall see face to face. Now I know in part; then I shall know fully, even as I am fully known." – St. Paul [37]

I remember years ago when I worked as the VP of Marketing for an insurance broker. I studied the markets relentlessly to know which carrier preferred what type of client, line of coverage, etc. On a bid for a large business, I elected not to send the proposal to a specific carrier because I knew that business was not in their appetite portfolio. We ended up losing the account to another broker who placed the business with that same carrier simply because they had asked! Reality changed and I missed it. It was an expensive lesson that I remember to this day.

During the process, I could not ever hear that carrier as an option. I had already closed the loop in my mind so it did not occur to me to check in. I thought I already knew so there was no possibility. Even the way we listen for possibility is impacted by what we think we already know. What we think we know is rooted in our winning strategies.

"The most erroneous stories are those we think we know best – and therefore never scrutinize or question." – Stephen Jay Gould, American paleontologist and evolutionary biologist [38]

What is a winning strategy and how do we challenge them? Let's say a winning strategy is a formula for how to win in life. It is a way you get what you want when you want it. For example, as a kid I learned having the right answer and being a good student was a way to win attention, kudos, and approval. You can see it in play in my earlier example. Having the right answer about which carrier is doing what blinded me to checking in. Ultimately, it was more important to be right than it was to be successful. (Not that I could see it at the time!)

Some people win attention by the opposite strategy—not doing well in school, goofing off, or self-identifying as the black sheep. It really does not matter what strategy you choose; it matters if it brings you what you think you want. We all have strategies we use, time and time again, because well, they do win. However, no strategy wins all the time. We lose resourcefulness when we attempt to apply the same strategy over and over in different contexts. It is like the expression *if the only tool you have is a hammer, everything looks like a nail.* The same applies to winning strategies.

If you look at your life, I bet you can identify at least one winning strategy you have been operating in, probably since you were young. Look for patterns in your relationships and reactions. Take a moment to look at your life from an observer's point of view, without judgment or defense. What can you see? Where do you automatically go in your head when you believe things are working out?

You cannot challenge what you cannot see—so begin by noticing.

Ask yourself:

1. What assumptions am I making?

2. What have I already decided is true about this person or circumstance?

3. What if that is not true or not the whole truth?

4. What else could be just as true or even truer?

5. Take a moment to listen to your internal conversation.

CURRENT REALITY CHECK: Did you identify a winning strategy of yours or were you immediately drawn to be right about someone else's winning strategy? When was the last time you learned something from your team? Are people regularly bringing you their ideas and perspectives or have you unconsciously created a culture of compliance?

9

The Leader Having Ears to Hear

Leaders are generous listeners. They are aware of their own internal conversation and diligently seek to align it with God's conversation about themselves, others, and circumstances. Listening both externally and internally provides a platform to encourage, edify, and build up others as well as to receive learning and correction from others.

What we commonly call listening is just waiting for my turn or selectively parsing the data only for what I want or expect to hear. Generous listening begins with recognizing the internal competition that is always present. Notice when other people are talking or even if you are by yourself reading, you are also talking in your head. Can you hear it? We all have internal conversations going all the time. I call mine the *internal editor*. The *internal editor* is always communicating and it has a lot of opinions. While someone else is talking, it is also talking. It is agreeing or disagreeing, liking or disliking, judging, editing, or ignoring. My internal conversation may be about something completely different from the original intent of the message. Maybe I am going over what I have to do later today. Maybe I am thinking about a sick child or a conversation that I need to have later that I am dreading.

My internal conversation sometimes is about myself. I am talking to myself about myself. What am I saying? I am saying *that was awesome of me* or maybe *I'm so stupid.* Or *I can't do this* or *I wish I were somewhere else.*

My internal conversation may also be about other things like *I can't believe they said that!* or, *I knew they didn't care. People don't like me. They are judging me. I bet they are thinking that I am a burden.* Oh wait, those last few are about me again. See what happened there?

There are always several conversations going on at any one time:

- the one you are having out loud with the other person

- the one they are having out loud with you

- the one that you are not saying out loud to them

- the one they are not having out loud with you

- the conversation that you are having about the conversation

- the conversation that you live in about yourself and others etc

Before you even have a conversation, notice what you are already saying to yourself about the person, the situation, and the results. Often we just have both sides of a conversation and leave the other person out completely! Part of generous listening is being aware of and noticing the multiplicity of conversations that are always present.

Our internal conversation has not only to do with how we hear but what we hear or listen for. Consider it like radar. When radar was first developed, it was designed to detect solid objects. And it did. However, it did not detect wind or other weather conditions. Does that mean that the wind and the weather were not there? Of course not! It just did not show up on the radar at first. I assert that we unconsciously tune our own internal radar to pick up certain things and as a by-product—it does not pick up other things.

> *"What is critically important to realize is that what we 'hear' or 'listen for' determines what we say, which in turn, determines our actions, which in turn, determines our future….the culture of an organization lives in conversation, and more specifically, in an aspect of conversation called 'listening.' It is this listening that forms the superglue of the culture, and it is already present before anyone in the organization speaks."* – Dr. Barbara Fittipaldi, author, President & CEO of Center for New Futures consulting and executive education firm [39]

What is she saying here? What are you hearing? If our listening determines our response, in the form of feelings and actions which then determine our future, how important is it then to examine our listening? What if we are missing critical data? How would we begin to discover our own radar?

Several years ago, my husband John and I were planning on having a few friends over for brunch on a Saturday morning. He got up and said, "I'm going to go downstairs and get everything started."

"Okay, great. I'm going to take a shower and wash my hair, then I'll be down," I replied. Well, forty-five minutes later, I headed downstairs. My internal conversation was fraught with stories about how John was probably upset that I took so long, frustrated he was doing the bulk of the prep and even judging me as vain because I spent so much time on my hair and makeup.

When I got to the kitchen, John said, "There you are!"

What I heard was *It's about time! Why did it take you so long? What's wrong with you?* So I immediately began defending myself, explaining what I was doing and why. He looked puzzled. He asked, "Babe, what did you hear me say?"

I stopped. I thought for a minute and said, "I heard you say why did you take so long and what's wrong with you."

He smiled. "No love, I was just happy to see you. All I said was 'there you are,' as in, yay! There you are!"

I learned a great lesson that day. Even though I understood the idea of listening filters, I had an opportunity to actually experience how they operate. There is a vast difference between having mental assent to a concept and living out the truth of it in real life. It is one reason I love transformational training; it gives people the opportunity to catch themselves being *themselves!*

Our thought life affects our listening. What thoughts do we give energy or value to? When I am listening to someone else, how might I be filtering his or her communication? For example, if I am saying *I already know that* either out loud or in my head, I am not really listening to everything being said. I am listening only to what I think I already know. Another way I might filter my listening is through my own assessments or judgments: *that's right/wrong, I agree/disagree, or that's good/bad.* On the other hand, perhaps I am listening through what I think should or should not be said or happen. All of our filters impede connecting with who is really there.

As leaders, we have a responsibility to manage our thoughts, to steward them towards the bigger vision of the organization and to provoke greatness in our teams. Consider the admonition of St. Paul:

> *"For though we live in the world, we do not wage war as the world does. The weapons we fight with are not the weapons of the world. On the contrary, they have divine power to demolish*

strongholds. We demolish arguments and every pretension that
sets itself up against the knowledge of God, and we take captive
every thought to make it obedient to Christ."[40]

He is speaking in a faith context, asking us to elevate our awareness
of the spiritual realm. Whether you consider yourself a person of
faith or not, consider the possibility of another realm, an invisible force
that influences the visible. Notice these conversations are referred to as
strongholds; strongholds that set themselves up against the knowledge of
God. They have a life of their own. Have you ever experienced a
conversation, either internal or external, having a life of its own, taking
you places you did not intend to go? Taking captive is war language.
It reveals the internal battle against the strongholds that reveal themselves
in conversation.

> *"If anyone has ears to hear, let him hear. Consider carefully what*
> *you hear," he continued. "With the measure you use, it will*
> *be measured to you — and even more. Whoever has will be given*
> *more; whoever does not have, even what he has will be taken*
> *from him."* – JESUS [41]

Jesus uses this phrase "if anyone has ears to hear, let him hear" over
fifteen times in the New Testament—so clearly He is not referring
to physical ears. Our *ears* are a reflection of our willingness to receive the
gift of another person in the moment.

Here are some common listening filters, adapted from Barbara
Fittipaldi's work [42]. Begin to notice when they are at play:

1. Assessment – voting on what we hear—that's good/bad, right/
wrong etc. If I hear something that I assess as bad or wrong, I give myself
permission to withhold my participation. We do not get to choose

whether or not we assess, just what we do with our assessments.

2. Listening for what we already know or are familiar with so that we miss or throw out what does not fit into that belief. If what I see or hear fits, I pay attention to it, if it does not fit, I ignore it. When we reduce all the input into what we already know (which is a past-based orientation), we automatically limit possibilities for the future.

3. Description – the way it should look, i.e. family looks this way, job looks this way, etc. It is as if we have a perfect world, perfect spouse, perfect boss, perfect children, and even a perfect self (and more) living in our heads. You will notice it by the number of *shoulds* and *shouldn'ts* you use every day. This filter naturally looks for blame. Whose fault it is that this situation or individual is not how it/they should be?

4. Personal – these are my thoughts and my feelings and everyone naturally sees things the same way. It causes me to live in unspoken expectations with others because it never occurs to me to clarify something that is obvious to me. How often have you thought *if I just explain all the data, they will come around to my way of thinking?* Only to discover that even with the same data set, people do not always see things the way you do!

Consider that *it* is thinking and you are having the thoughts. *It* is the culture. We are steeped in so many conversations, as if they are true. Test: if they are your thoughts, then stop thinking. Go ahead. How did that go? Consider what is really going on is that the thoughts have you. After all, your thoughts and feelings are not unique to you. Notice how you hold them as if they are *yours*. If they are just thoughts and feelings, then we can choose how we have them. It is as if we are choosing to internally tune in to a certain station on the radio. We can always select another station.

These are *human* conversations and we are all constantly entertaining them, or not. They are environmental and cultural conversations. They predispose us to the past and unless we start becoming aware of them, we miss possibilities in the moment. The filters naturally produce resistance and subsequent withdrawal of our participation in life. When we notice them, we can turn down the volume on them, make them less significant, and begin listening to what else is present.

By noticing the _way_ you listen and how you are naturally filtering your listening, you will start to have more room for inquiry and new choices.

CURRENT REALITY CHECK: *What patterns have you noticed in your internal dialogue? How would you describe the predominant attitude or mood of those conversations? When was the last time you checked in with someone about what you heard them say?*

10

The Leader as Adaptable

Leaders adapt to different people, beliefs, and situations. They are flexible; assessing the situation and the people involved and adapting themselves accordingly. As listening opens up, we naturally become more flexible. We hear new possibilities for action that previously did not occur to us.

Being adaptable is an integral part of connecting to others. Our natural tendency is to unknowingly expect people to process, communicate, and articulate the way we do. (It is, of course, the right way!) This unconscious expectation creates rigidity.

Flexibility stems from curiosity. As we maintain a learner's mind, we find more space for knowing people. We can flex our style to communicate whether people prefer the bottom line, lots of details, the big picture, or an emotional context.

This trait applies to the market, new technology, and the economy as well. Great leaders pay attention to trends, feedback from the people on the ground, and changing technology as well as their own vision for what is possible.

The more generously you listen, the more flexibility you can access. The assumptions and assessments that we live in about how things should be, how other people should be, how you should be, influence our flexibility. Notice if your assessments throw you into a right/wrong, good/bad, or should/shouldn't conversation. When they do, you probably experience more frustration or need to control or fix others. Human beings naturally resist change and gravitate towards what is predictable. Predictability is connected to our innate survival instinct. Flexibility allows us to be present in the moment and discover additional resources that are available now.

Saint Paul demonstrated his flexibility as a leader when he wrote this verse to the people in Corinth.

> *For though I am free from all men, I have made myself a servant to all, that I might win the more; and to the Jews I became as a Jew, that I might win Jews; to those who are under the law, as under the law, that I might win those who are under the law; to those who are without law, as without law (not being without law toward God,* but under law toward Christ*), that I might win those who are without law; to the weak I became as* weak, that I might win the weak. I have become all things to all men, that I might by all means save some. Now this I do for the gospel's sake, that I may be partaker of it with you.* 43

I remember once working with a leadership team of twelve people. During a training session, we were discussing how to motivate different people, to call out the heroic in the various team members. The CEO said, "I just go around every day and let people know I could do their job better than them but I don't have the time!"

As I surveyed the faces in the room, I could tell this was not an exaggeration. So I asked, "How many of you are motivated by this statement?" Three out of the other eleven people raised their hands.

The man sitting next to the CEO put his head in his hands, then looked up and said, "I have been coming to work every day for the past two years thinking I was on the verge of being fired."

The CEO looked shocked and replied, "You are one of the most valuable members of the team." The man almost burst into tears. All of the energy expended every day caught up in the conversation about what *might* happen had built up to a breaking point. Flooded with relief, he was able to see how much energy had been siphoned off into his internal conversation and how it had affected not only his daily experience of life but also the bottom line. His hero had been in retreat!

It did not occur to this CEO to be flexible, to adapt to the different people on his team. He assumed that what motivated him would naturally motivate everyone else as well. This blindness to other choices and possibilities creates not only relational disconnect but also a type of rigidity. His inflexibility was costing his leadership team valuable time, energy, and resources. Instead of focusing on their daily goals and objectives, potential was being diverted to manage unnecessary internal conversations.

Whatever motivates you may or may not motivate your team. If you are unwilling to shift your way of being with people, you will certainly miss out on the synergy available with all members of the team.

"If you don't like change, you are going to like irrelevance even less!" – General Shinseki, retired U.S. Army General 44

CURRENT REALITY CHECK: How would you describe your team or your family or your community? Are you aware of how you approach each individual? Do you have a variety of personalities and talents or have you unwittingly assembled an army of clones?

11

The Leader Having Direction

Leaders are focused and purposeful. The things of this world do not distract them. Their vision brings clarity and purpose. It creates a clearing for others to join in and participate.

> *"One of the best paradoxes of leadership is a leader's need to be both stubborn and open-minded. A leader must insist on sticking to a vision and stay on course to the destination. And he must be open-minded during the process."* – SIMON SINEK, AUTHOR AND MOTIVATIONAL SPEAKER [45]

Living in the paradox of both courageously moving towards a vision and maintaining a willingness to listen to others along the way is a necessary tension. It is tempting to forge ahead without hearing counsel. Sometimes it is necessary. Sometimes is it lethal. Discerning the difference between a distraction, a word of wisdom, tenacious pursuit of a vision, and an ego trip requires intentionality, focus, and humility.

It is easy to be swept up in the day-to-day distractions, the voices of your critics or competition, or simply the echo of your insecurities. Maintaining focus takes intentionality. It requires stewarding your resources towards the bigger picture, even when circumstances cloud the view.

In 2016, I was in Taiwan working with a corporate client. The conference center was set in the mountains, beautiful views all around. The first day was clear and sunny. From the deck outside the training room, I could see the trees all the way up to the top of the mountains in the distance. The next day was rainy and foggy. From the same vantage point, all I could see was fog and mist. I thought, *this is just like life. I can't see the mountain, but I know it's still there. The fog and mist obscure my view and somehow bring their own beauty.* Circumstances come and go—vision remains. The circumstances themselves may even serve to reinforce my persistence, if I stand clearly on my purpose.

The clarity of my vision creates a space for others to participate. It provides a set of constraints, in the best sense of the word, that allows for freedom and creativity. The space I make for other people to enter into the journey alongside me is a mark of a great leader. Consider the invitation Jesus created with His disciples. They all participated, to the point of martyrdom for most of them. Even today, people all over the world still participate in the space He made for us to come together.

How clear is your vision? Do you allow yourself to get distracted when everything is not falling into place the way you imagined it would? Notice if your vision includes people or just you. If you create a space for participation, what can happen? Listen for how you relate to others; if someone else brings up a new idea or possibility do you hear it as a threat to derail the vision or diminish it? Can you hear the distinction between having the vision and having a way that the vision comes to pass?

In recent studies on motivation and drive, Daniel Pink, business author and speaker, offers the following recipe for motivating employees to participate in the corporate vision:

Autonomy: People want to have control over their work.

Mastery: People want to get better at what they do.

> **Purpose:** People want to be part of something that is bigger than they are. [46]

Often the term motivation is reduced to a mechanism of punishment or reward. Psychology has defined two types of motivation. One is extrinsic in that an external reward is given for certain behavior. Essentially, like tying a carrot to a stick to make a horse run. Intrinsic motivation is an internal reward for behavior. So rather than paying for the next person's coffee in line at Starbucks to have someone give me a pat on the back—I do it because I enjoy the experience of surprising and delighting a stranger, brightening their day. It establishes a sense of well-being within myself for no reason other than I enjoy it. It feeds my hero.

This extrinsic or carrot and stick type thinking around motivation has proven ineffective and even counterproductive for employees. It is necessary at times but it will not create a culture where people willingly go the extra mile to make something memorable happen for your customers or other employees. Intrinsic motivation taps into people's internal drive, their bigger purpose in participating, the hero side of their being. It is what lasts and makes a lasting difference in an organization or a family. When there is a lack of 'visioning' in the organization, people cannot see how mastery of their area supports the bigger vision of the organization. All they see is the carrot.

Often we have a vision and have already decided how it will best be implemented. It's natural to have all of the steps laid out and just start looking for people to fill in the blanks and do their part. When other people come to the table with their own ideas and methods, it can seem like an interruption. Others then show up as a problem instead of a possibility. When people are problems, it is easy to have contempt for them and relate to them from our belief about how we think they should be:

i.e. resistance. Think about the difference between a compass and a map. A map is only relevant in known territory. If you are committed to an unprecedented future, unmapped territory, then you use a compass, not a map. Vision is a compass.

"Where there is no vision, the people perish..."
– ANCIENT PROVERB 47

Most organizations, families, and relationships crumble for lack of vision. We are designed to operate from vision, to have purpose, to see how our contribution fits into a large whole. Great leaders communicate vision over and over. Maintaining this level of clarity and focus requires, as St. Paul called it, keeping eyes on the prize. It is the relentless reorientation of self and others in pursuit of something bigger than any one person.

"Do you not know that in a race all the runners run, but only one gets the prize? Run in such a way as to get the prize. Everyone who competes in the games goes into strict training. They do it to get a crown that will not last; but we do it to get a crown that will last forever. Therefore, I do not run like a man running aimlessly; I do not fight like a man beating the air. No, I beat my body and make it my slave so that after I have preached to others, I myself will not be disqualified for the prize." – ST. PAUL 48

Beating our bodies is not very inviting in the moment; however, the unprecedented requires discipline. In any area of life where we refuse discipline, we invite disaster. As a leader, we are continually called to model discipline of thought, speech, and action while remaining vulnerable, authentic, and connected. You cannot possibly over-communicate vision.

Leadership calls for grounding both self and others into a foundation for the vision. Who are we together? What is our purpose? How do we activate our values in practical daily interactions with each other and with our customers? Most leaders have a clear vision yet neglect to orient the team, over and over again, about who they are and what they are doing together. Essentially, they forget to inform everyone else of the vision! The orientation of the vision provides a container for people to put their learning in. Without it, people will naturally drift towards their own interpretations, ideas, and agendas. Because people and circumstances are dynamic, leadership requires a type of repetition; grounding yourself repeatedly as well as ensuring your team is grounded in the driving principles of your organization. This orientation creates the foundation for powerful and congruent action. Direct the vision to your team, not just the task.

CURRENT REALITY CHECK: Is your vision driving your daily decision-making or do you find yourself in continuous fire drills? How often do you check in with your team on how they see their individual role in the bigger vision? In what ways do you communicate purpose and values? Based on results, how well is your team oriented? Do you invest the time in grounding yourself daily?

12

The Leader as an Environment of Transformation

Leaders are 'environments' of transformation for others. They emanate transformation. Their disposition or attitude reflects a humble heart. Leaders are aware of their position and their influence and are responsible for their impact on others.

Consider what it means to be an environment for transformation. Ask yourself, *am I an invitation for people to step into their greatness or do I spend my energy manipulating or controlling, feeling like it is my job to make someone do something? Am I feeding my hero and the heroes around me?* What is your conversation about the people that you are leading? What is their purpose? What is your purpose? What do you assume people are up to? Notice how your assumptions influence the results that you have. Consider that every person has a spark looking to be ignited— both inspired and inspiring. Be clear upfront that you have high expectations for who is there, what they are committed to, and what you are doing together.

"Miracles: You do not have to look for them. They are there,
24-7, beaming like radio waves all around you. Put up
the antenna, turn up the volume - snap... crackle... this just in, every
person you talk to is a chance to change the world..."
– HUGH ELLIOTT, AUTHOR [49]

Scientific studies have determined a correlation between expectation
and performance. It is called the Pygmalion Effect or Rosenthal Effect.
It is the documented effect of higher expectations leading to better
performance. The name comes from the Greek myth about Pygmalion,
an artist who fell in love with his own statue. Even if you imagine
your words are consistently encouraging toward the people you lead,
remember your expectations are also communicated through *presence*,
attitude, and mood.

Presencing is not simply words or actions. It is the environment
created by your way of being. It is a dynamic proposition. Yes, it includes
thought, speech, and action but it is not just those things. There is a
spirit, mood, or disposition that draws the best out of people.
It is the environment created through attitude and engagement. It is
an impartation. And we all can offer it in our own unique expression.

"Make a careful exploration of who you are and the work
you have been given, and then sink yourself into that. Don't be
impressed with yourself. Don't compare yourself with others.
Each of you must take responsibility for doing the creative best
you can with your own life." – ST. PAUL [50]

Humility is a sense of groundedness in who you are. It comes from
the Latin *humilis* meaning lowly, humble, literally on the ground,
from 'humus' meaning earth. In the last section, we examined groundedness or orientation. Where is your identity grounded? Are you allowing

the results, others, or your own internal fears and insecurities to dictate your identity? Try this on: you are steadfast in your identity as Beloved, with nothing to protect and nothing to prove. Humility has been described as that particular state of grace where you know exactly who you are.

> *"Therefore let him who thinks he stands take heed lest he fall. No temptation has overtaken you except such as is common to man; but God is faithful, who will not allow you to be tempted beyond what you are able, but with the temptation will also make the way of escape, that you may be able to bear it. Therefore, my beloved, flee from idolatry."* – St. Paul [51]

I love the juxtaposition of verse 14 with the two just prior. Whenever we think we are standing on our own, we do not need others or God, we are indulging some form of idolatry. Often we relate to idolatry as something only relevant in the Old Testament yet are blind to how self-sufficiency itself can easily become an idol and separate us from God and others.

We were not created to live independently of relationships with God and others. When we become our own source, we naturally run out of resources and live in scarcity. It is contagious. Left with only ourselves as a resource, we do not readily see the gift of others, the provision embedded in even the most challenging circumstance or the possibility to ask for what we need. This level of independence pushes people away and communicates, *I don't need you.* When leaders unknowingly send this message, they model it to their teams, families, and communities. If you can identify the predominant attitude in any group, you can trace it back to leadership. Attitude always follows leadership.

The irony is we can readily identify other people's attitudes but tend to be blind towards our own. I was facilitating a marriage workshop in Zambia in 2016 and the couples began sharing their cultural views on sex. It is common for a woman to be told, as part of her preparation for marriage, she is not allowed to ever say no to her husband if he wants to have sex.

I was asked what I thought of this custom, since there were differing views on it between the men and the women in the room! The men were complaining about the women's attitudes and the women were complaining about the men's. I asked, "Well, what attitude does this belief set up in the men?" There was a long pause then one of the men spoke up and said entitlement. "Yes, I can see that. And what attitude does this belief invite in the women?"

The women starting sharing how it felt like they were being forced and they did not have a choice. "What attitude is that?"

They responded with resentment.

"So, does anyone in here like being forced or not feeling like they have a choice in life?" A resounding NO came from everyone. "What would it be like if both parties owned their attitude and made choices based on your vision for your marriage?" Immediately the couples began coming up with new ways to have conversations, create agreement, and enjoy the sexual expression in their marriage.

We cannot shift what we cannot see. Start by noticing the tenor and context of your internal conversations. Write down what you notice and you will get immediate insight into your attitude. Once you have a sense of what lives internally, look externally and see how the environment mirrors your private conversations. Consciousness creates the possibility for choice. When you become aware of your contribution to the environment, you can begin to make necessary changes to realign your attitude to your values and vision.

CURRENT REALITY CHECK: Describe the overall attitude of your team. Ask yourself, how have I contributed to what I see? When someone new enters your space, how does he or she experience the culture? Have you asked them? Does the culture inspire growth? Are people stepping up into leadership and growing or do people need to leave to advance?

13

The Leader Utilizing Resource & Responsibility

Leaders stand in the confidence that everything can be provision. Provision is always available, constant, and abundant, regardless of circumstances. With this view, leaders are responsible for discovering what is wanted and needed to continue to transform. They are willing to account for their impact and live a lifestyle of repentance. In other words, a practice of being willing to change your mind about people and circumstances; to take on other perspectives. Responsibility means to promise in return, to answer. It is a response to the weight of your glory. It's not a *have to*, something you are forced to do, or do not have a choice in. It is a get to, a privilege and a joy because of who you are and why you are here.

> *"Not everyone looks at obstacles – often the same ones you and I face – and sees reason to despair. In fact, they see the opposite. They see a problem with a ready solution. They see a chance to test and improve themselves. Nothing stands in their way. Rather, everything guides them on the way."*
> – RYAN HOLIDAY, AUTHOR [52]

How do you typically respond when circumstances surprise you, when things are not the way you thought they would be? Are you automatically angry, depressed, frustrated or withdrawn? Or do you slow down and wonder what is available or possible now? Whatever the results are, they are great communicators! Notice how we relate to the results—what do they communicate back to me, as a leader, about my participation? The responsibility of freedom includes the willingness of a leader to actually see and account for their contribution to the results. Leaders model attitude. When we live responsibility, more possibilities open up. This is key to transformation—it opens up committed action steps and is a critical part of discovering the current reality. If I believe every moment contains the resource I need, I will locate the resource in the face of any circumstance. This is the manna of our daily lives—His constant provision and care.

In 2004, I was invited to meet with a CEO of a large dental practice. When we sat down, he began explaining all of the problems with the organization. The marketing team was not communicating with the sales team, the board was frustrated with the results, and the dentist/office staff relationships were strained. When he was done, I asked, "How long have these breakdowns been happening?"

He said, "Oh, for years!"

Then I asked, "So why do you want it this way?"

"What?! I don't want it this way! That's why I'm talking to you!"

"First, I'd like to explore why you've tolerated it for so long and what you're getting out of the status quo. You're the CEO so you are an integral part of this system." No, I was not fired. We started exploring his contributions to the state of the organization. From that vantage point, we were able to create new actions and re-engage his leadership team to create something new.

"If people are still externalizing their problems, they create, in a sense, 'externalized visions,' which amount to a kind of change strategy for fixing problems which they have not seen their part in creating. Only when people begin to see their part in how those forces might evolve does vision become powerful. Everything else is just vague hope. ...most visions that management teams come up with are superficial. Even if they embody a lot of good thinking, they're still a product of fragmented awareness..."
— FROM *PRESENCE* BY PETER SENGE, C. OTTO SCHARMER, JOSEPH JAWORSKI AND BETTY SUE FLOWERS [53]

There is an inverse relationship between reasons and results. Try this on next time you do not have the results you intended. Note the image below. Create a list of the results you *do* have on the right side.
On the left side, list all the reasons you do not have the results you were aiming for. For example, if your sales goal for the year was $100,000 in new business but at the end of the year, you only have $80,000, you have $20,000 worth of reasons for not meeting the goal. Reasons like: it was a stretch goal to begin with; the team was not communicating; the market changed; the competition was too tough etc. If you are being honest, you will find most of these reasons were already in your mind *before* the year started.

REASONS   # RESULTS

Often when working with a team, I'll ask:

1. **What are the goals?** This is an opportunity to hear from each person. Often the team is working on different goals without even knowing.

2. **How confident are you that you will reach the goal?** I ask for a percentage from each person. It lets me know what conversations may be lurking underneath the surface.

3. **What reasons or excuses do you already have in your mind about how this will not work?** Exposing the existing beliefs ready to sabotage success is a great way to address them before it is too late. Often the reasons or excuses point to valid concerns that need to be discussed. Once out in the light, they can be addressed before moving forward.

As a leader, if I view life from the perspective that God is who He says He is, then I will be confident to locate provision in the midst of even the most difficult and painful circumstances. It requires a type of certainty, not in what will happen, but in who I am in the midst of whatever is happening. As I engage situations and people through the certainty of an abundant Father, I begin to surrender my selfish expectations and trust I have everything I need in the moment.

> *"Every blessing is too good for us to receive if we measure it by our unworthiness; but no blessing is too good for God to give, if we judge of it by his surpassing excellence. It is after the nature of a God of love to give boundless blessing. If Alexander gave like a king, shall not Jehovah give like a God?"* – CHARLES SPURGEON, 19TH CENTURY BRITISH PREACHER AND AUTHOR 54

What if God is always providing? Even the breakdowns are a provision in connecting to current reality!

When I am anchored to this reality, I can receive feedback from others as well as interpret organizational results as feedback. When my confidence is secure, I can hear when my actions or attitudes need adjustment in alignment with my vision. Repenting, accounting, and going again are natural occurrences in any healthy relationship.

For example, I have been told several times by different people in my life that I can come across as aloof, insensitive, and arrogant. At first, I resisted that feedback. I blamed, explained, and judged the source. Then it came back from a different source. And then another one. And another one. What was up with that?! The feedback just did not fit into my fantasy version of myself. I seem okay to me, I mean, I know my intentions and they are good ones. At some point, I decided that if I were honestly committed to being the type of person I already thought I was, I would want to hear where and when and how I missed that mark. Therefore, I started listening. I did not like what I heard. It exposed motives like making myself superior, thinking I was smarter than other people, wanting to look good to others, being in control. There was truth in every one of them.

After beating myself up for a while about it, I started a Seek and Destroy mission on my judgments, bad attitudes, and any other stuff I thought was a problem. There was a lot. It became a consuming task, so consuming, in fact, that I had to actually start pretending it was working. In other words, I stopped wanting to see what was really there so I just morphed it. For example, if I am condescending to my husband and he calls me on it, I find a way to make it about him. Like he did not understand, he was defensive, he was not listening. I denied, avoided, pushed back, and pretended. Sound familiar? All this time, I was leaving a mark. Well, more like road kill, but still a mark.

The strategy of attempting to identify and destroy all my flaws became exhausting. It was as if I had signed up for a continual lesson in de-motivation. While I was busily focusing on what was not working, I missed everything that was working. It was like being stuck in a bad movie and unable to leave the theatre. It occurred to me that recognition was something that I could do and perhaps in that space of awareness, I could actually choose. I could choose whether or not to indulge my self-absorption or to consider others. I could leave the mark I was designed to leave or I could settle for road kill.

When we give in to our self-absorption, our fears win out. We seek to protect ourselves, cover our butts, keep from being too invested, too excited, too passionate, or too alive. We might be rejected, we might fail. Somehow it seems like these disappointments might take us out of the game. Therefore, we work to minimize or mitigate the possibility of future disappointment. Mitigating disappointment is a great way to diminish your legacy. It looks like not giving 100%—*after all, 50% is probably good enough.* There are so many good reasons to hold back! *No one appreciates me. I don't know what 100% looks like. If I'm doing good stuff at 50%, why kill myself putting forth all that extra effort?* Plus, we gain the added benefit of having a built-in excuse when things do not work out—*well, if I had really given 100%, it would have turned out differently.*

There are so many ways to attempt to avoid or prevent disappointment. If we are paying attention, we can hear it in our language. Words like *might, kinda, try,* and *maybe*—all reveal our internal struggle, ambivalence, and even despair. Malcolm Gladwell in his book *Outliers,* defines mitigated speech as "any attempt to downplay or sugarcoat the meaning of what is being said."55 If we are busy sugarcoating our lives, our impact, our value, the mark we are leaving may just be a faint pencil scratch instead of the bright splash of yellow paint that is possible.

Mitigating disappointment is ultimately a strategy for pain management. We are desperate to avoid the pain of life so we pretend, resign, run, and hide—and all the while, the mark we are meant to make becomes at best the pencil scratch or at worst it looks like road kill. It is often not the pain that destroys our legacy, it is the denial, the avoiding it, that ultimately numbs and then kills. Contrary to what our fears tell us, we can actually enter into the pain in such a way that brings healing—both ours and others. We can be heroic. There is the pain that heals and the pain that persists. And it is not about the pain itself. It is about how we view our legacy, the unique and precious gift of our life and our responsibility to share, give it, impart it.

With all our tendencies to mitigate, avoid, and hide, it is easy to become confused about what is possible. If being human means I cannot be perfect and being human means I am drawn to be perfect, then how does that impact the mark I am making day in and day out? I became curious about what being human actually meant and how it worked out in a practical sense. Maybe this sounds crazy but I began to wonder if our humanity was both the reason we could leave a mark on someone's life and what interfered with leaving a mark. I am not advocating indulging in, excusing, or resigning to the lesser parts of our nature. I am suggesting that they are part of what allows us to operate with compassion, empathy, boldness, and resolve. It is the judgments we hold about our humanity that sabotage our legacy.

To look at it another way, our judgments blind us to our purpose. We create hostages with chains of unrealistic expectations for others and ourselves. We tend to swing between resignation and rebellion, unwilling to be with the ambiguity that comes with being human. We make prisons, step inside, and then forget that we hold key on a chain around our necks—like when we cannot find our glasses as they sit perched on our heads. Our judgments blind us to our beauty.

What is the beauty that you are here to impart? What is it that lights you up?

What do you want to give/share/contribute?

When I was traveling in South Africa in April 2012, I had the privilege of facilitating a workshop for women with my dear friend Amy Maxwell who collaborates with me in our nonprofit GAP Community. We were working with sixteen women from the township of Kayamandi, just outside of Cape Town. In the midst of sharing life with these amazing women, we exchanged stories of joy, pain, loss, betrayal, sacrifice, and beauty. I was moved to tears at the commonality of our struggles, victories, and longings. As I sat and wept, a seventy-two-year-old woman named Nonzame Dotwana stood up and walked across the room. She came to me, wiped my tears, and held my face in her hands. I was impacted by profound grace, care, and intimacy. We connected in our tears; touched something that was invisible yet tangible. Love moved and danced among us and brought beauty from the ashes of our suffering and longing. Two months later I got an email from a dear friend, Nompi, in Kayamandi, letting me know that Nonzame had died. All I could think of in that moment was how glad I was that I got to meet her and I recognized I am marked. For life. And it only took a moment.

When was the last time you were marked? What happened? Who marked you? Recall a time recently. Allow yourself to consider the impact on your life. How would you describe the mark? Was it the result of extraordinary effort or the mark of daily discipline and everyday courage? How long did it take? A moment? An hour? A week? Were you grateful? Embarrassed? Inspired? Sometimes we are marked by giant blaring amazingness. I have been blessed to be a recipient of these types of marks—many times.

As leaders, we have a responsibility to lead ourselves well, to allow ourselves to mature, be inspired, hear from others, be humbled, persevere, and rise over and over again.

Leaders who resist responsibility never mature. They may become great at throwing tantrums and getting their own way but miss out on the synergy and learning available by leading responsibly.

Notice if your organization frames accountability as being held accountable versus people taking initiative and responsibly accounting for their results themselves.

When people are operating from a responsible context, they naturally communicate if they may miss a deadline, a meeting, or if they need help on a project. If accountability is limited to being caught or called on the carpet when things are not done, the culture becomes punitive. It also invites an environment where people hide or minimize their mistakes instead of bringing them to the team for learning and solutions.

When accountability is lacking, people stop expecting others to do what they say they will do, when they say they will do it. This creates a conspiracy of mediocrity where people stop calling others on not keeping their word because they do not want to be called on for the same. Eventually, it trickles down to clients and customers because it is a context people operate in. It becomes the norm to break your word and excuse it.

As we explore our own mindsets around leading and leadership, we will also keep an eye out for common pitfalls.

CURRENT REALITY CHECK: What are the results in your organization telling you? When you identify a problem, are you also able to see your contribution? What payoffs and what prices have you been settling for up until now? How does your team investigate both what works and what has not been working?

14

Leadership Kryptonite – Four Pitfalls

When navigating with vision as your compass, it is helpful to anticipate some common traps along the journey. Just as the Leadership Distinctions are daily disciplines, Leadership Kryptonite weakens our superpowers. They are continuous temptations to lower the bar, let yourself or others off the hook, or settle for less than what is possible. We are going to explore four of the subtlest and consequently deadliest snares. Pay attention to your internal conversation as you read through them. Notice if you start making excuses about a time you did or did not do something addressed here. Relax. They are common pitfalls precisely because almost every person on the planet falls into one at one time or another.

#1 AVOIDING DIFFICULT CONVERSATIONS

As you explore your beliefs, notice how your beliefs about which conversations will be 'difficult' influence the way you engage others. Notice how they contribute to resisting the conversations completely. When you resist or put off having a conversation that you have predetermined will be difficult, what reasoning or story do you use? Do you tell yourself *they won't listen* or *last time I tried to have a conversation, it didn't go well or they don't care,* or something else along these lines?

Why is this important and what does the topic of difficult conversations have to do with leadership? Jack Welch, a well-known CEO of General Electric and considered a great leader, once said he measures the success of his day by the number of difficult conversations he engages.[56] When you think about difficult conversations in your own life, what happens? Do you get nervous? Excited? Avoidant? If you are spending energy avoiding potential conflict, you are probably guaranteeing conflict!

Here are some tips adapted from the book Difficult Conversations. Distinguishing Impact from Intent:

- You know your intent but are unaware of your impact.

- You make assumptions about your impact based on your intent.

- Others know your impact but are unaware of your intent.

- Others make assumptions about your intent based on your impact.[57]

"The conclusions we draw about intentions based on the impact of others' actions on us are rarely charitable…we attribute intentions to others all the time." – DOUGLAS STONE, BRUCE PATTON AND SHEILA HEEN, AUTHORS [58]

Recall times when you have invested in justifying your intention to the exclusion of accounting for your impact. Impact is part of the *current reality* for individuals in relationships.

We are automatically drawn towards focusing on or defending our intentions. After all, they are so clear to us! We tend to miss the actual impact of our words and/or behavior. If we are willing to live in the reality of our impact on others, to be curious about it, explore it, examine it, then our leadership will naturally develop. We will have the invaluable opportunity to receive feedback so we can course correct.

Another way to live responsibly as a leader is to consider every breakdown as an invitation to investigate your contribution rather than simply assign blame. The good news is owning your contribution paves the way for something new. If we cannot see our part in contributing to a problem, we will be powerless to affect change in that area. We are left powerless because the only hope we have is in changing others. As attractive as that sounds, it is outside of the realm of our control.

> *"Our work, our relationships, and our lives succeed or fail one conversation at a time. While no single conversation is guaranteed to transform a company, a relationship, or a life, any single conversation can. Speak and listen as if this is the most important conversation you will ever have with this person. It could be. Participate as if it matters. It does."* – Susan Scott, Fierce Conversations [59]

Notice whether you or your team tend towards complaint versus contribution. For example, someone might say they get mixed messages from management and if asked "have you talked to them about your experience" they may respond, "no, it's no use." When a culture does not communicate responsibly, it sets up a victim, villain, and rescuer dynamic where people see themselves and everyone else in one (or two) of these roles. The blindness to personal contribution ensures all breakdowns, frustrations, and problems stay in place. There is a benefit in always having someone else to blame; it alleviates personal responsibility and the need to change. Blame creates its own comfort zone, which is an attractive place to hide when faced with the discomfort of change.

Here is an example. When I was the marketing manager for an insurance brokerage, I would have proposals prepared for commercial clients outlining options for their coverage plans. My assistant would help put the portfolio together and I would take it to the client. Often, I would be in a hurry, rushing to get out the door and I would just grab the binder and get in the car. Once, as I sat in front of a client, I realized there were several mistakes in the presentation. I fumbled to explain and correct what was presented. When I returned to the office, I wanted to blame my assistant for not being thorough, let her know how embarrassed I was and how unprofessional we looked. When we sat down, I pointed out the mistakes and asked her what happened. She said, "Honestly, you are often in a hurry and I feel intimidated by you so I was afraid to ask you questions or be perceived as slowing you down by having you review it before you left." I was shocked. I had no idea that was the environment I was creating and immediately could see my contribution to the breakdown. As I was willing to own my part, it made it easier for her to own hers and ultimately for our dynamic to change.

It is easy to overlook certain types of contributions. Being unapproachable (or intimidating) can easily contribute to a breakdown. Procrastination is another contribution—the longer you wait to address an issue, the more entrenched it becomes. It allows more time for the situation to deteriorate; to create more hurt feelings or stories.

As a leader, an integral part of responsibility is owning my contribution. Responsibility is not blame; it is the opposite of blame. Some people collapse blame and contribution and end up just blaming themselves instead of owning their part. Blaming, either yourself or someone else, arises from a victim mindset.

Acknowledging your contribution makes addressing a breakdown or difficult conversation a powerful opportunity for mutual learning and connection. Consider, if you are clearer about the other person's contribution than you are about your own, you may want to get clear before you address a breakdown.

Of course, if you do not want to be clear, you may be willing to settle for other types of payoffs. Think of engaging conversations you would label as 'difficult' as slaying your own personal dragons. Pick up the phone, set the appointment, make the coffee date.

CURRENT REALITY CHECK: On average, how many difficult conversations do you have on a weekly basis? Monthly? If you cannot think of the last one you had, chances are you are unaware of your impact in critical ways. Decide now to take action on a conversation you have been putting off.

#2 CORDIAL HYPOCRISY

Cordial hypocrisy is defined as the strong tendency, because of loyalty or fear, to pretend that there is trust where there is none; being polite while privately indulging cynicism or distrust.[60]

Here are some common ways this dynamic shows up in community:

- Creating workarounds to avoid interacting with someone.

- Gossip disguised as prayer.

- Privately holding yourself as superior.

- Talking to others about someone's struggles without sharing with them directly.

- Making excuses not to speak directly to someone with whom you have an offense.

- Sharing your offense with others instead of speaking directly to the person who has offended you.

Cordial hypocrisy is a wall of silence. The only thing that gets in is what people want to hear; the only thing that gets out is the status quo.

This is the number one mechanism that undermines seeing the current reality in an organization. It is in every relationship, culture, and family.

Cordial hypocrisy is an attitude of heart. It is the way we set up relationships and live into them. It ultimately diminishes intimacy and depth.

> *"Don't you understand that discipleship is not only about being right or being perfect or being efficient? It's about the way you live with each other. In every encounter we either give life or we drain it. There is no neutral exchange. We enhance human dignity or we diminish it."* – BRENNAN MANNING, AUTHOR [61]

Cordial hypocrisy undermines dignity—both yours and the other person's. Ask yourself, what are the conversations you have been avoiding and with whom? How long have these conversations been living in the background, under the table? What would it take for you to bring these conversations into the light and vulnerably share your assessments with others? What kind of community could be built if we were willing to live this way?

Our maturity as leaders and as believers hinges on the way we own and address our own cordial hypocrisy. It is everywhere in families, businesses, churches, and friendships. Remember, it is driven by loyalty or fear, so it can easily slip into place with people you love and are afraid of losing.

One way to interrupt the natural cordial hypocrisy in any organization or group is to make a regular practice of giving feedback and inviting assessments. Feedback is simply someone's experience. It is not the *truth*, however, it is true for them. It is distinct from advice or psychological diagnosis; it is related to impact.

An assessment is a thought, feeling, or experience. It is usually kept private, not entertained out loud. Remember the value of exploring the emotional context?

People are motivated and can adapt quicker when they can give and receive feedback in real-time. If you wait until the annual review or the monthly meeting, you are probably:

1. Losing valuable time to make course corrections.

2. Frustrating your high performers.

3. Discouraging data from the field to be sent back up the organization.

Feedback can include your work product, results, attitude, mood, or communication. Feedback is invaluable to a healthy team and healthy leadership. Here are a few of the benefits:

- People get a sense of their impact.

- Promotion of alignment and integrity.

- Providing what is missing in relationships and current reality.

Teams need to be oriented on how to give and receive feedback. I encourage leaders to make time for the team to share feedback and assessments. Sometimes it is helpful to have a format for sharing so people stay on track. Remember, if the conversations were easy, they would already be happening. Here is a way I like to structure an assessment session, adapted from Dr. Fernando Flores' work:

1. Get the group together and explain the purpose and value of honestly sharing assessments. As the leader, set the table for participation. Since there is a power differential in the room, make sure the team knows they will not be sanctioned or fired because of something they share in this session.

2. Ask who would be willing to receive an assessment? Who is willing to give one? Check in to see if people want to receive but not give—this is a great opportunity to investigate underlying conversations and attitudes.

3. Once the team is clear and ready to fully participate, ask who will be willing to go first or invite someone to give you, as the leader, the first assessment. One way is to use this script to assist the team in staying on track:

   a. Go to someone in the room and deliver your assessment by saying: (Name) my assessment of you is...

   b. The person receiving the assessment listens attentively, without speaking.

   c. When the person giving the assessment is done, the person receiving asks, "Is there anything else?" then waits.

   d. When the assessment is complete, the person receiving the assessment says, "Thank you for your assessment. I appreciate your honesty. I would like to have a further conversation with you about this later."

   e. The person giving the assessment says, "You are welcome."

Afterwards, both parties sit back down. I recognize this may sound like boot camp, however, the stark nature of the structure is helpful to keep people focused on simply hearing the feedback. There may be other assessments coming to them or they may have other assessments to give. No one needs to complete the conversation during this meeting. Practice listening and receiving. Allow yourself to notice and consider what was shared. There is nothing to do or to fix right now. The team is free to set up a time to have follow up conversations at a later time.

Notice any defensiveness that may arise, in yourself or in others. Remember, attitude follows leadership. The more open and humble you are, the bigger invitation you are for your team to give and receive feedback. If you find yourself getting defensive, just acknowledge it out loud and release it.

Once it is established as a normal part of communication, you will find people who want to engage openly will stick around and those who do not will self-select out of the group. As mentioned in the beginning of the book, transformation is a violent process. As you begin to make changes, it will disrupt the organization. The good news is, as you establish and reinforce a distinct culture around the values, mission, and vision of the organization, your team will also gain confidence and clarity around what to expect and how to participate.

As leaders address the cordial hypocrisy in themselves and their organizations, it opens the door to keeping short accounts with others. Regularly releasing and moving off of the things we tend to hold onto is a discipline of a great leader.

> *CURRENT REALITY CHECK: How often have you thought to yourself: it is no use even trying to talk to (fill in the blank)? Then when other people come to you with the same complaint, do you create a workaround instead of addressing your concern? When was the last time you exercised courage when giving feedback to a peer? A superior? A staff member?*

#3 GRUDGES, BITTERNESS, AND RESENTMENT

What does it mean to move off of or release something? It means to relinquish your grip and focus on past situations, conversations, and assessments about yourself or others. In other words, live out the discipline of forgiveness.

When you indulge a grudge against someone, it overflows into other relationships. It is an attitude of the heart and like any attitude, it is imparted to others. Continually holding onto grudges or resentments leads to bitterness. It is like the Pop Up you see every time you think of someone or see their name on your phone or in your social media feed.

Bitterness is not a flattering word; it is not something most of us would readily own. So how do you know when you are walking in bitterness, in unforgiveness? Remember, our self-flattery blinds us to the state of our own heart. We tell ourselves *I'm not that kind of person.* We decide that bitterness is bad and wrong and, of course, do not want to associate ourselves with whatever is bad/wrong. So how can you see something that you may not want to see and what would be the benefit of seeing it after all? Bitterness leaves a distinct mark. It leaves suspicion, entitlement, anger, revenge, and over time, indifference. We stop caring. Notice where and with whom you have withdrawn your care. Maybe it is a boundary or maybe it is an excuse not to go again.

Releasing what you have been holding onto is an opportunity to put aside your judgment, expectation, and create something new with the relationship. It might be something you experienced or just something you imagined. Maybe it is the way you have filled in the blanks for missing data. Here is an opportunity to decide to have your conscience and your internal conversation align with what you say matters most to you in the relationship. You get to choose to let go of what you have been keeping score about in your relationships. Remember, keeping score fosters resentment and self-righteousness.

Resentment is a waste of energy. Resentment rarely hurts those it is directed towards, it acts like a boomerang, coming right back to you. As a leader, your personal energy management is critical. All of your communication, including facial expression, tone, mood, and body language flow from your energy.

What does resentment create?

–Bitterness and anger.

–Justification for holding back and self-protection.

–Adherence to the pain of the past.

By continuing to resent, you are wasting your emotional, intellectual, and physical energy on an activity that is unproductive for an effective leader. Getting rid of resentment ultimately means declaring that you are done feeding your resentments. It is not about forgetting it or pretending it never happened but choosing to reduce its significance. It is declaring something happened and it may have felt important at the time but I am not allowing it to determine who I am.

Here are a few examples of things we can get stuck on:

- Our agendas

- Our perspective

- Our judgment

- Our comparisons

- Our stories

- Our need to be right/defend/control

- Our expectations

- Giving up on people

- Using people

- Our offenses/hurts

- Our guilt

- People 'hearing' us

- Getting rid of our resistance

The discipline of forgiveness is not typically viewed as a real-world leadership skill. The practical value of forgivingness in a modern leader creates substantive change in not only the leader, but also their teams and allows for creativity, growth, and innovation. In any expression of leadership across sectors (e.g., business, government, or civil) forgiveness is a powerful force for change. Recent developments in neuroscience as well as current events, point to its significance in a leadership context. It is a confessional process where you humbly acknowledge what you have been holding onto, imagining, or allowing to interfere with a relationship. It is an opportunity to bring your private conversations into the light where they can be sifted and sanctified.

> *"For if you forgive men when they sin against you, your heavenly Father will also forgive you. But if you do not forgive men their sins, your Father will not forgive your sins."* – JESUS [62]

Jesus clearly weights the value and need of walking in forgiveness. It is the key to freedom. It is the language of the humble.

> *"Forgiveness is the name of love practiced among people who love poorly. The hard truth is that all of us love poorly. We need to forgive and be forgiven every day, every hour—unceasingly. That is the great work of love among the fellowship of the weak that is the human family."* – HENRI NOUWEN, DUTCH CATHOLIC PRIEST, THEOLOGIAN, AND AUTHOR [63]

People intuitively understand that leadership is not a transactional endeavor; it is a relational endeavor at every level.

Here is some homework for you. As you read the last passage, who came to mind? Maybe it was one specific person or a few people. Ask yourself, *what conversation do I have the most energy around?* Take the opportunity to call or visit that person and have the conversation with them. If you have trouble knowing how to start the conversation, consider this structure as a way to sort through what needs to be said.

Releasing Script

1. Tell them what you have been holding (be specific).

2. Let them know what you may have made up or how you may have filled in the blanks.

3. Declare you are releasing what you have been holding, what you have made up, and any judgments attached to it.

4. Check in with them—what are they hearing and feeling?

5. Listen to them; what is their experience?

6. Stay connected and vulnerable in the conversation.

Before you continue with this book, take the opportunity to release what you have been holding onto with at least one other person. Take a risk! The world is in need of courageous leaders willing to embody the reality of forgiveness.

Journal what you noticed in the exchange: what you felt, what happened, what surprised you, and anything else that stands out to you about the conversation.

CURRENT REALITY CHECK: Make a list of people you have not forgiven and the offenses you are holding and notice what

*you notice. What themes or patterns emerge? What story are you
fortifying about yourself? About others?*

#4 MAKING DECISIONS FOR PEOPLE

Your primary role is to lead not to give advice or find answers for others.
Remember Friedman's definition of being a non-anxious and principled
presence in the midst of reactivity and anxiety? Your role is to draw
out or provoke their leadership by listening for their orientation. Feed
their hero. You cannot do that if you are asking and answering your
own questions. Telling people what to do is valuable in a crisis. For the
long-term, it pays to inquire and listen to where someone is coming
from, what they are seeing, and perhaps more importantly, what they are
making the situation mean. Remember the Zeigarnik effect from Chapter
4? Asking questions and leaving people to come up with a response
creates an open loop in their thinking. The brain will continually come
back to the question as it attempts to find resolution. This generates
self-initiated insight and learning, which tends to stick, as opposed to
advice, which may be easily disregarded.

Giving answers and solutions, correction without inquiry, and allowing
blame shifting fortify a culture of correctness. By correctness, I mean
people focused on getting it right, not getting in trouble, and doing what
they think you want them to do. While you may experience decent
short-term results, you will suffer many surprises later as people's true
characters emerge under stress or crisis. Most people take the path of least
resistance simply to survive their day and conserve energy. When you
give answers—instead of invite inquiry—you play into this strong default.

Edwin Friedman writes, "the colossal misunderstanding of our time
is the assumption that insight will work with people who are unmotivated

to change."[64] Increasingly in our culture, the entry-level workforce is becoming less and less mature. This means less inclined to assume responsibility for their emotional world and their own choices and to express themselves without blaming. Most organizational leaders find themselves teaching ethics, etiquette, responsibility, as well as specific job skills. The temptation is to step in and parent the employees. You know, help them out by telling them what to do, giving them answers and, in a sense, doing their work for them. Naturally, employee orientation is integral to successful onboarding programs. I am suggesting the way we orient our staff is more of a context, an expression of culture, than a checklist.

There is a vast difference between caretaking and caregiving. Often leaders slip into caretaking, which is doing something for someone they could do for themselves. If you look at the original definition of the word 'caretaking' it involves overseeing the property of an absent owner. When we are caretaking another person, the attitudinal implication is they are absent. They are not really able to manage their own life. It feeds a victimology which reinforces relieving tension as the highest good. It is a formula for blame. Caregiving is authentic care for another person which often includes allowing them to struggle and develop their own character in the process. If you are not sure whether you are caretaking or caregiving in a relationship, ask yourself, *is this person becoming stronger or weaker as a result of my involvement?* Remember, the focus is on feeding heroes not enabling poor performance or underdeveloped character.

As a leader, focus on your own integrity and presence. Allow the presence you bring to model responsibility, curiosity, and creativity. Instead of deciding for someone else what they can handle, afford, or endure—consider standing with them for what they say matters in their life and watch them rise.

CURRENT REALITY CHECK: Take note of how often you correct someone without inquiring first into his or her thought process and listening for ownership. Notice if asking questions seems like it will take a lot of time and so you just bottom line your communication with what you want. Spend a week just noticing and journaling what you observe. Ask yourself, is my team taking more and more ownership of their realm of responsibility? Are they motivated to learn, grow and change or are they focused on getting it right?

15

Tuning Your Leadership Radar – 5 Superpowers

How was your homework from the prior chapter? Did you do it? Did you think about doing it? Did you ignore it? Participate in your leadership journey the way you want your team to participate in the mission, vision, and values of your organization.

If you did the homework, chances are something beautiful occurred and I would love to hear about it so send me an email with your story!

These five superpowers are practices, daily disciplines. If you make regular practice of each one, you will continue to transform your leadership in powerful and surprising ways. Think of it like going to the gym. If you go regularly, you will see results. If you hire a personal trainer or a coach, you will see faster results. Let these practices be your personal trainer and coach.

PRACTICE #1 – INTENTIONAL GRATITUDE

It is easy to feel grateful when life turns out the way we want it to, when people are how they are supposed to be, or when we feel like we are winning. Practicing gratitude as a discipline requires a transformed mind.

I am not suggesting you deny your experience or live in a Pollyanna fantasy world. I am inviting you into an attitude that, even in suffering, makes room for thankfulness. It is a broadening of life's experiences, not a pigeonholing.

Years ago I lost a business partner. What I did not realize at the time was I also lost a friend. Their view of friendship hinged on us working together, heading in the same direction. When our interests diverged, the relationship all but ended. In my grieving, I disciplined myself to stay grateful for the fifteen years we had together, for the variety of experiences we shared, for what I learned, and for the people we served. I am not suggesting it was a perfect or painless process, I am saying it was a valuable one. By choosing gratitude, I was able to keep resentment from taking hold and eating away at my future.

> *"To be grateful for the good things that happen in our lives is easy, but to be grateful for all our lives – the good as well as the bad, the moments of joy as well as the moments of sorrow, the successes as well as the failures, the rewards as well as the rejections – that requires hard spiritual work…As long as we keep dividing our lives between events and people we would like to remember and those we would rather forget, we cannot claim the fullness of our beings as a gift from God to be grateful for."*
> – HENRI NOUWEN, DUTCH CATHOLIC PRIEST, THEOLOGIAN AND AUTHOR[65]

Practice full gratitude. Be intentional in every situation. As you do, allow yourself to receive a greater experience of life with others. And do not keep it to yourself! Webster's definition of appreciate is "to acknowledge the full worth of."

Being appreciated by another person is a powerful human experience. When people understand they are appreciated, they go the extra mile, work smarter, share ideas generously, and appreciate others in return. Appreciation is a necessary component of feedback. Mature leadership thrives and develops with relevant and time-sensitive feedback. As leaders, we often see the areas needing adjustment or correction and forget to make appreciation equally important.

Take the time to write a note, make a phone call, take someone for coffee, or invite him or her into your office and let them know specifically what you appreciate about them. Details matter. The more specific you are willing to be, the more valuable for the recipient.

In 2006, I had the privilege of facilitating a four-day youth training in South Africa. We had twenty-six teens participating from every ethnicity and background imaginable. Much of South Africa is still healing from the apartheid movement so this was an incredible occurrence. On the evening of the third day, a white teenage boy stood up and confessed to several of the black teens in the room, "When I first came here, you were invisible to me. After the first day, I could see you. By the end of the second day, I could hear you. Now, I can feel you." Speaking these words of repentance and gratefulness, he broke down and wept. It was a healing moment provoked by an awareness of the gift of others as they poured into his life. And he poured back.

Gratitude is what grounds us to the reality of our connectedness with God and others. When we practice thankfulness, it allows us both to give and receive with an open heart. We pour out and allow others to pour in.

PRACTICE #2 – MINIMIZE REGRETS, ELEVATE VISION

Think about all of the internal conversations that minimize your gratitude. Maybe they sound like regrets that cycle and recycle in your mind: things you did, things you did not do, things that were done to you or not done for you. Notice how much of your life is tied up in shame informing you how bad or messed up or inadequate you are every day.

Take out a piece of paper, draw a line down the middle, title the left side Regrets and write them out on the left side of the paper. Use a real paper and pen, not your phone or laptop. Psychology has shown that writing increases learning better than typing.[66] Pause and write.

When you are done, consider how much energy you spend on a daily or weekly basis recycling or reviewing these conversations. Even though it will not be a scientific measure, at the bottom of the column, write out a percent of your time that seems accurate for all of these thoughts. What did you come up with? 50%? 30%? 85%?

Now title the other column *Vision*, write down the things in life you are most passionate about, the activities that make you come alive, what you believe you are here on the planet for. Think about when you seem to have unlimited energy—what are you doing? Who are you with? Keep writing and allow yourself to fully express everything that is there.

When you are done, look back at the percentage you wrote on the first column. Now write the balance of that number totaling 100% on the bottom of the *Vision* column. For example, if you wrote 50% on the left side, write 50% on the right side; if you wrote 30% on the left side, write 70% on the right side. Here is the reality—you only have 100% of your energy each day and whatever energy you spend on your *regrets* is not available for your *vision*.

What do you think life would be like if everyone had an additional 15-45% of their energy freed up to pursue their vision? How would your family be? Your business? Think of your energy as power. If you are giving power to the past, how much is left for the present? For the future?

What would our world be like if everyone lived out of their vision and purpose? Would we have less competition and more appreciation? Would the hungry be fed and the naked be clothed? Would the orphans know family?

> *"Hide not your talents, they for use were made. What's a sundial in the shade?"* – BENJAMIN FRANKLIN[67]

We all have power and we are all using it for something. Sometimes we use it to reinforce our perceived limitations. Sometimes we use it to propel ourselves into a new future. When vision is elevated, purpose is served, passion comes alive and perseverance is a natural by-product.

PRACTICE #3 – GET GROUNDED, BE PRESENT AND PRACTICE SELF-CARE

Start each day with a grounding ritual. It might be meditation or prayer. It might be writing. It might be a long walk, doing yoga, or stretching your body. Or all of the above! Move your body with intention.

In Tim Ferriss' book *The Tools of Titans* over 90% of all CEOs he interviewed practice some form of meditation daily.[68] One ritual I recommend adding is noticing the automatic assumptions that wake up with you each morning. Write them down so you can study them, challenge them, and investigate them—all without judgment. Find a ritual that brings you energy and focuses your intention for the day. Start in the morning before the onslaught of phone calls, texts, emails, and meetings. Carve some time for yourself as an expression of both self-care and care for others.

This includes paying attention to your physical health and the way you treat your body. Pay attention to your cravings, what you eat, and when you eat. What are your current eating and exercise habits? Would you recommend them to your team? To your family?

Notice your breathing. Is it shallow, fast, deep? When you breathe, does your chest move? Your belly? Your ribs? Your ribcage is designed to move in all directions, not just out and in. Begin to notice and vary your breathing. Notice if there are times you hold your breath. What are you telling your body? How is it influencing the people around you?

Stay curious about your health. My good friend Todd, who is a fantastic trainer and coach, was having problems with blood clots. If you travel for work, this can be quite concerning since airplane flights exacerbate clotting. In pursuit of his health, he took the 23andMe genetic and health testing and discovered he metabolizes warfarin much faster than the average person does. Later that same week he was hospitalized for a serious clot and was able to tell the doctor the results of his genetic testing. His doctor increased his dosage to account for Todd's metabolism. It may have saved his life. This is self-care—staying curious and continually learning about your own body and what it is saying to you so you can be fully present.

> *"Real generosity towards the future lies in giving all to what is present."* – ALBERT CAMUS, FRENCH PHILOSOPHER, AUTHOR, AND JOURNALIST[69]

Our internal conversations are either in the past, the present, or the future. Notice where you like to camp out. If it is the past, you may be resistant to change. To be clear, there is nothing wrong with the past. It can be a powerful teacher, an anchor for provision, a resource for what is next. Releasing it has to do with the way you relate to it in the moment. Do you allow what has happened before to inform what is possible right now? Does your last experience with someone dictate all future experiences? When you are in a new situation, are you imaginatively gridlocked because you are emotionally entangled in a past conversation or experience?

If you tend to live in the future, you might be spending a lot of energy feeling anxious or worried. Again, there is nothing wrong with looking to the future, it is a natural part of casting vision and opening creativity. It can also be an escape, a fantasy, a way to avoid doing forensics on current reality. Are you exhausted at the end of the day, attempting to continually be prepared for what might happen? Do you find it hard to enjoy a success or look constructively at a failure? When you give your word, do you tend to lose track of commitments in the moment because you are somewhere else in your mind?

The practice of being present is a discipline. Remember, the present moment is ripe with provisions. What does it take to be fully present with another person? What will you need to release to actually see and hear them? How many other internal conversations compete for your attention in the moment? What expectations are creating blinders for you?

Allow yourself to quiet the internal chatter, to calm the chaos inside and create a space in your heart to receive the gift of another. You will find as you practice being present you have much more energy at the end of the day.

Decide to be curious during the day. Consider curiosity as an expression of wonder. Wonder is a trait most often found in small children as they are learning and experiencing the newness of the world. At some point, the newness wears off and the need to already know and move on takes over. Allow your grounding to bring you clarity and confidence for the day.

Being grounded and staying curious helps us to remain neutral. One of the keys to leading well is developing the ability to remain neutral, i.e. avoid getting hooked into a battle of right and wrong over some point, a power struggle, stuck in the content, and losing context fast. Ask yourself, *how invested am I in my position? Am I trying to prove something? Can I present my points as possible ways of looking at issues instead of the way it is?* You can stand for what you believe in without being so attached to it that you cannot hear others. Instead of being captured by someone else's suspicion, negativity, or resignation, choose to remain positive. Champion them, be on their team! Be passionate about the new possibilities they can create in their professional lives.

After about thirty days you will begin to notice a new rhythm. Perfectionism will lose its grip on your thought life. Find your practice, one that works for you and do it, daily. Breathe. You will find you have more space to be with people and with yourself.

PRACTICE #4 – CREATE YOUR PERSONAL LEADERSHIP DECLARATION

What does your personal leadership declaration sound like? After going through this book and examining your own style, tendencies, strengths, and blind spots, what are you willing to declare as the future of your leadership from now on?

It is time to create your personal leadership declaration. Think of it as a statement about who you are committed to be for the people you lead.

Begin with brainstorming all of the characteristics that you are committed to embody as a leader. What is your full vision for your leadership? Write them down and keep writing until you have everything out on the paper. Go ahead, do it now. I will be right here waiting.

Now, look at what you have written. What three or four words stand out to you? What seems the truest of your heart to lead? Consider the experience you are committed to creating for the people around you. Is it trust, passion, hope, strength, empathy? What is it?

Pick the top three characteristics of a leader and place them into this declaration:

I AM A _____, _____ ____, *AND*

_____ *LEADER.*

Say it out loud to yourself several times. Decide to own it, to live into it. Share your declaration with your team so they know what to expect and how to provide meaningful feedback in the context of your commitment. Write it down and place it somewhere you can see it every day. Review it in the morning during your prayer or journaling time. Use it as an anchor to keep you tethered when circumstances threaten to rock your world.

PRACTICE #5 – GENERATE CONVERSATIONS FOR ACTION

Using your personal leadership declaration, write down ten specific actions that you will take to live out this declaration. What ten actions can help you get to that declaration?

Include timelines for each action, be sure to include actions that you can start right away within twenty-four hours, forty-eight hours, seventy-two hours, next week, two weeks, three weeks, and a month from now. The actions must be specific, include a deadline (by when will it be done) and a challenge for you. Effective action planning connects to our emotional life—what would be a risk? What would create something unprecedented in your life?

As you prepare your list of actions, consider what promises you will make and to whom. A promise is a way we send ourselves forth into the world. Webster's 1828 Dictionary defines promise as:

"In a general sense, a declaration, written or verbal, made by one person to another, which binds the person who makes it, either in honor, conscience or law, to do or forbear a certain act specified; a declaration which gives to the person to whom it is made, a right to expect or to claim the performance or forbearance of the act." Your promises connect you to others. They create a legitimate expectation for the other person. The expression 'your word is your bond' is true, it is how people know you and it is what builds your reputation.

We make promises all day long, even if we are not using the word promise. We set up expectations and create connections based on our word. When you write down an action step, think about who will be impacted by this action. Be willing to share it with them and establish a promise.

The format I use looks like this:

#	ACTION STEP + EMOTIONAL CONNECTION	WHO ELSE + BY WHEN

Invite your team to create specific action steps around shared goals and values. As people begin to account for their commitments and re-up when needed, synergy develops. You can easily see where people are aligned, where resources are needed, and how workloads are distributed.

Finally, make a practice of reviewing your practices! Take inventory semi-annually at a minimum and ask yourself *Is this working? What are the results? What needs to change? Where am I falling short?* As you involve others in your commitments, you will be receiving feedback from them as well to help you see what you cannot see on your own. For example, I know when my husband says, "Hey, you've been short with me lately" chances are good I am not practicing self-care. I need to go outside, stretch, take a walk around the block, and change my physical space. When I do not keep a deadline, I ask myself, *what am I resisting and why?* Then I can re-anchor into my leadership declaration and remind myself who I am and clarify my purpose. As you implement these new habits, you will notice some practices seem easier or more natural than others. Do not be discouraged! They are intended to cause you to stretch yourself into creating new patterns of behavior.

16

Leave It All on the Field

When I asked the women I worked with in Afghanistan what were
the hardest things to believe about themselves, we heard responses like:
"that I am confident," "that I am beautiful," "that my voice matters,"
and one woman shared "that God has created me for something good."
One of my most memorable relationships there was with a woman
named Halima. Barely five feet tall, she showed up in one of my train-
the-trainer classes like a joy bomb! Her passionate commitment to
the women of Afghanistan led her to create a non-profit there, offering
free classes
in leadership, time management, decision making, and women's rights
as well as providing a space to speak freely, commune, and care for
one another.

When I asked her what she took away from the training classes she
replied, "When we open our soul's eye to look at each other, we can
see differently." Her stand and her words sparked something heroic in me
to continue my work there in the face of threat and instability.

We can roll through life without stepping into these moments—
either being open to receive them or generate them for others. We can
camouflage our gift so it blends in with the background noise and
becomes less noticeable. We can lower the expectations of others to the

point where we can stay safely in the confines of our comfort. Cozy. When we are tucked into a pile of pillows, we cannot feel the blows of life. We can be cushioned to the point of numbness. While numb keeps us safe from the hits, it also keeps us from leaving our mark.

When we are truly alive, we are both making marks and marking others. We are giving and receiving. There is an exchange happening that edifies both parties. It feeds our inner hero and sparks our vision. Sometimes it is scary, but most times it is just plain amazing.

So take some risks—real risks—way outside of your normal behavior but still perfectly congruent with your internal desire. The way I see it, if we acted on many of our internal promptings to care, we would regularly go beyond ourselves into the vast field of otherness. Think about it. If every time you just thought about giving someone a hand, an encouraging word, a hug, or a gift you actually followed through and did it, what would happen? What would the path of your life look like? What happens when you do?

> *"The way is full of genuine sacrifice.*
> *The thickets blocking the path are anything*
> *that keeps you from that, any fear*
> *that you may be broken to bits like a glass bottle.*
> *This road demands courage and stamina,*
> *yet it's full of footprints!*
> *Who are these companions?*
> *They are rungs in your ladder.*
> *Use them!*
> *With company you quicken your ascent."*
> – RUMI, 13TH CENTURY PERSIAN POET AND SUFI MASTER[70]

I believe that we are all naturally drawn to connect in meaningful ways with one another. We long for connection and think of ways to make it happen. We are compelled to use our actions, words, and talents to make a unique mark on this earth and the people in it. How do I know? Notice how common depression, anxiety, self-hatred, and disconnection have become in our world. These shadows are evidence of a longing unfulfilled. When there is unforgiveness, depression, and loneliness it speaks of these missed connections. If the connection did not matter in the first place, we would not be affected by its absence.

The powerful truth is we are designed for connection, created to make a mark everywhere we are—in our homes, in our communities, at our workplaces. In a recent book, *Firms of Endearment*, the author makes it clear: businesses committed to making a mark, creating value for all of their stakeholders—customers, employees, stockholders, vendors—are more profitable, have lower turnover, deeper customer loyalty, and higher employee morale. In every area of life, when we are true to our design to make that difference and leave that mark, beautiful things happen.

The best part is we are often unaware when we are leaving a mark. We are keenly aware when someone else marks our lives, yet when we are truly operating in our gifting, it is almost invisible to us. When we are truly present with another, we are not thinking about ourselves so we cannot notice our own mark.

What if everyone started getting intentional about noticing when they are marked? What if that heightened awareness created an environment where people believed that they had the opportunity to make a difference with someone else and looked for those opportunities? What if we were open to allowing other people to mark us? Imagine waking up in the morning and instead of starting the litany of complaints running through your head as you prepare for your day, you consider all the people that you are able to exchange life with that day. Your family. Your co-workers. Your customers. Strangers at the coffee shop. People at the grocery store. And you actually get excited. You find yourself centered, curious, anticipatory, wondering, and ready to take the chance to get to know who you are with, in any moment. You would be calling out the heroic in those around you.

Maybe you are thinking that I am suggesting some Pollyanna-ish version of life that does not exist. That is okay. It is just the resistance talking. Of course, there are going to be struggles, people having a bad day, you having a bad day—count on it. Does that mean it is not worth giving yourself to the possibility? You might risk losing a little cynicism, gaining a bit of courage, surprising yourself by going beyond what you thought was possible.

Remember the movie *Pay it Forward*? It was a call to give yourself, do something great for someone that maybe you did not even know. Pay it forward—be generous. A few years ago, my husband and I went to dinner at a local restaurant. When it was time for the check, the waitress told us that someone had paid our bill. We still do not know who or why, they were just paying it forward. Living your legacy now, engaging your heroic adventure is like that. It is an awareness that we are always making an impression so how about leaving the one that reflects the best version of ourselves and touches the lives of others? We can do that every day, in every interaction. We can even do it when it seems as if someone else is leaving road kill in our lives. The circumstances never determine our character or our mark. We can always choose.

Choose the assumptions you live in, about yourself or others. I choose to assume people long to make a difference, to be championed into the most heroic and powerful version of themselves. While it has generally been my experience, I know it is not categorically true.

I also notice when I operate as if it is true I find more people who live in this conversation. Rosamund Stone and Benjamin Zander say it this way in their book *The Art of Possibility*:

"…The practice of enrollment is about giving yourself as a possibility to others and being ready, in turn, to catch their spark. It is about playing together as partners in a field of light…the steps to the practice are:

1. Imagine that people are an invitation for enrollment.

2. Stand ready to participate, willing to be moved and inspired.

3. Offer that which lights you up.

4. Have no doubt that others are eager to catch the spark."[71]

Think about someone who has marked your life—a teacher, a coach, a parent, a grandparent. How long ago was it? I remember my mom teaching me how to sew, my grandfather teaching me to ride a horse, my dad teaching me to draw—all marks. I remember when I was at college in D.C. at Georgetown University. One night I was sitting outside on the steps near the library (the fishbowl, as we called it), feeling really depressed and worried about my younger sister who was across the country from me. I had my head down in my arms when someone walked up to me and said, "Hey are you ok?"

I said, "Sure."

He patted my arm and said, "Keep the faith," as he walked off. I had no idea who it was and I never saw him again on campus. I will never forget it. A complete stranger cared enough to stop and risk judgment, rejection, or reaction to encourage me. Our exchange let me know somehow that everything was going to be all right. That simple encouragement opened the door for me to hope, to persevere, and to stand. It carried me through one dark night and into the many future days and nights.

This moment occurred for me because someone I did not know chose to be courageous. What is courage? It has been defined by poets, writers, soldiers, and statesmen over the history of mankind. What is courage for you? Maybe it is the extra time you take to listen when you would rather move ahead with you own plan. Maybe it is doing what you know is right, even if no one else agrees. Maybe it is using your voice, speaking your truth in the face of cynicism, despair, or hatred. Every one of us has courage—we are born with it. Now whether or not we use, exercise it, develop it, and practice it—that is another story. I love G.K. Chesterton's quote on courage:

> *"Courage is almost a contradiction in terms. It means a strong desire to live taking the form of a readiness to die. "He that will lose his life, the same shall save it," is not a piece of mysticism for saints and heroes...a soldier surrounded by enemies, if he is to cut his way out, needs to combine a strong desire for living with a strange carelessness about dying. He must not merely cling to life, for then he will be a coward, and will not escape. He must not merely wait for death, for then he will be a suicide, and will not escape. He must seek his life in a spirit of furious indifference to it; he must desire life like water and yet drink death like wine."* [72]

Each one of us has had those moments where we have been marked by someone else's courage and willingness to risk. Moments that gave us hope, turned our life around, brought courage, provided resources, lifted our spirits, or illuminated our path. So many moments. Be that moment for someone.

Now imagine what if each one was captured, memorialized,

and written down? What if you were the one who made the mark
and you never knew? What would it be like for you to find out?
Consider how powerful these expressions of acknowledgment and
gratitude could be in your life and in the lives of others. Businesses,
schools, and organizations leave marks as well. What would it be like to
know what organizations were leaving a mark in their community
or with their stakeholders?

Maybe it sounds compelling, exciting, or even breathtaking!
Maybe it sounds laborious, impossible, and ridiculous. I know it is easy
to stop caring. Sometimes it comes so naturally that we fool ourselves
into thinking it is true. We imagine that we can trade numbness for pain
when numbness is just a different kind of pain—the kind that kills.
All the lies we tell ourselves to keep the numbness in place: *it doesn't
matter, no one cares,* or *it won't turn out.* You know what? It is all true.
Sometimes it does not matter the way that we think it should, and
people, at times, do not care, or it almost never turns out the way we
want it to. Nevertheless, what is just as true, or even truer, is that there
are many times when it does matter; when people care deeply, and
when it turns out better than we could have imagined in ways we never
could have conceived. Keep going. In the midst of circumstances that
could bring defeat, our spirits find victory. Victory in the eternal game
where everything makes a difference.

Can we set our minds to navigate by the eternal game? Do we dare
to believe that while we physically waste away, our spirit is being renewed
daily? If we did believe it, we would know that each moment holds the
seeds of our legacy.

My friend in Afghanistan told me, "When I came to interview at the
office here, I could feel that God was in the hearts of the people in this

office. I was drawn to work here." What is that invisible ever-present reality that draws us to one another? You can see the mark you make on the lives of others by paying attention to who is drawn to you and why. Also, notice who you are drawn to and why. Take account of your relationships—what are the patterns you notice?

One final story: in January 2016, I traveled to Lusaka, Zambia, to do some outreach through my nonprofit GAP Community. While I was there I met a woman named Gladys. Gladys has nine children, seven are her natural children and two are her niece and nephew, whose parents died of HIV/Aids a few years ago. Gladys' husband left her in 2014. Oh, and Gladys is blind. She has been her whole life. Her husband is also blind. None of her children are blind, they range in age from six to seventeen. To earn a living, she and her children would wake up at 4 am and bake small rolls to be sold at the market. Her youngest would take Gladys to the market on two different buses across the city to sit and sell the rolls. The other children would all make their way to school.

In late 2015, Gladys decided she needed to further her education so she could make a better living for her family. So she found a school that taught a one-week class in keyboarding to the blind. The school was in a city about three hours away by bus. Gladys signed up for the class, boarded the bus, and traveled by herself to a city she had never been, to attend a class about something she was not familiar with. She did this out of her vision for her family. She stayed for a week and then returned. She began looking for work where she could use her new skills.

There is more to the story, of course. But let's pause here. Can you imagine for a moment what it would be like to be blind? If you are reading this book with your eyes, probably not. Could you imagine having nine children? Maybe you do not need to imagine because you do! If not, take a minute and let your mind wonder. Alternatively, perhaps you know what it is like having your spouse up and leave. Add all of these together and you get a glimpse of Gladys' life. But only if you also live in a third world country where the average monthly income is around $80 and your home is a made of wood, corrugated metal, and has a dirt floor. You know what is remarkable about this story—her attitude. Gladys' close friends say they have never really heard her complain or blame. She lives in a context of gratitude within a reality that is unimaginable to most people.

When I see Gladys and her family, they are all dressed in clean clothes and have great manners. All of the children, down to the youngest, will look you in the eye and engage you in conversation. Gladys herself is soft-spoken and clear. Being with her family is an extraordinary experience.

So, what makes one person rise in the midst of potentially devastating circumstances and another person crumble when their dry cleaning is late? I am not suggesting there is no room for grieving, sadness, or disappointment. Those are all real and necessary parts of the human experience. I am wondering, even in those moments, how are we relating to what has happened and what becomes imparted to those around us.

Is Gladys a leader, a hero? Certainly. She is a leader and a hero and she is feeding the heroes around her.

Maybe right now you are only leading yourself. That is a great and necessary place to begin! If you did not start your leadership journey by leading yourself, it might explain the gaps in your experience and on your team. It is not too late! Maybe you lead a huge team, family, or community. Wherever you are, take action. Feed the hero in yourself and others.

How do you build a legacy within yourself? What does your self-talk encourage, invite, provoke, and sustain? Are you aware of the constant communication you have with yourself? What if your self-legacy is what leaked out to others? What has been awakened in you?

Choosing from vision instead of circumstances or feelings is a form of courage. Choose to exercise the courage to act, to care, to go again. There will never be another _now_ like this one!

Endnotes:

1   Peter Koestenbaum, *Leadership, the Inner Side of Greatness,* (San Francisco: Jossey-Bass, Inc., 1991) derived from several chapters

2   Steven Pressfield, *The War of Art: Break Through the Blocks and Win Your Inner Creative Battles* (New York: Black Irish Entertainment, LLC. 2002) preface

3   William Glasser, *Choice Theory, a New Psychology of Personal Freedom* (HarperCollins e-books, 2010), 53.

4   Brainyquotes.com, "Francois de La Rochefoucauld", https://www.brainyquote.com/quotes/francois_de_la_rochefouca_126108 (accessed 28 Jan. 2018)

5   TED2014 March 2014 https://www.ted.com/talks/simon_sinek_why_good_leaders_make_you_feel_safe

6   *Forrest Gump,* dir. by Robert Zemeckis (1994: Paramount Pictures, 2001 dvd)

7   John G. Miller, *Flipping the Switch: Unleash the Power of Personal Accountability Using the QBQ* (New York: Penguin Random House LLC, 2006), 7

8   Daniel Coyle, *The Talent Code: Greatness Isn't Born. It's Grown. Here's How.* (New York: Bantam Dell, 2009), 60

9   Dallas Willard, Transformed by the Renewing of the Mind video series at The Carl Henry Center, February 2011

10   Daniel Coyle, *The Talent Code: Greatness Isn't Born. It's Grown. Here's How.* (New York: Bantam Dell, 2009), 34

11   Romans 12:2 (New King James Version)

12 William C. Taylor "The Leader of the Future", *Fast Company*, 31 May 1999, https://www.fastcompany.com/37229/leader-future (accessed 28 Jan. 2018)

13 Isaiah 55:8-9 (New King James Version)

14 Zeigarnik 1927: *Das Behalten erledigter und unerledigter Handlungen.* Psychologische Forschung 9, 1-8 https://en.wikipedia.org/wiki/Zeigarnik_effect

15 Lamentations 3:40 (New King James Version)

16 Chris Musselwhite, "Self-Awareness and the Effective Leader", *Inc. Magazine*, Oct. 2007, https://www.inc.com/resources/leadership/articles/20071001/musselwhite.html (accessed 26 Jan. 2018)

17 Soren Kierkegaard, *Provocations* (Walden, New York: Plough Publishing House 2002), 256

18 *Creatingminds.org*, "Thomas Edison", http://creatingminds.org/quotes/by_experts.htm (accessed 28 Jan. 2018)

19 Brainyquotes.com, "Simon Newcomb", https://www.brainyquote.com/quotes/simon_newcomb_205063 (accessed 28 Jan. 2018)

20 *Creatingminds.org*, "American Road Congress 1913" http://creatingminds.org/quotes/by_experts.htm (accessed 28 Jan. 2018)

21 Goodreads.com, "Harry M. Warner", https://www.goodreads.com/author/show/6453545.H_M_Warner (accessed 28 Jan. 2018)

22 https://www.pcworld.com/article/155984/worst_tech_predictions.html (accessed 31 Jan. 2018)

23 Frans Johannson, *The Medici Effect: Breakthrough Insights at the*

Intersection of Ideas, Concepts, and Cultures (Boston: Harvard Business School Press, 2004)

24 Cynthia Bourgeault, *The Shape of God: Deepening the Mystery of the Trinity*, disc 2 (CAC: 2004), CD, DVD, MP3 download

25 Thomas S. Kuhn, *Scientific Revolutions* (Chicago: University of Chicago Press, 1962), preface

26 Joel Arthur Barker, *Paradigms, the Business of Discovering the Future* (New York: Harper Business Press, 1992), 86

27 Joe Dispenza, D.C. *Evolve your Brain the Science of Changing Your Mind* (Deerfield Beach: Health Communications, Inc., 2007), 353

28 William Hutchison Murray, *The Scottish Himalayan Expedition* (London: J.M. Dent & Sons, 1951), 6

29 Edwin H. Friedman, *A Failure of Nerve: Leadership in the Age of the Quick Fix*, (New York: Church Publishing Inc., 2007) 91

30 Romans 5:3-5 (New International Version)

31 Frances Frei, Roy H. Williams "We Believe" video, (Austin, Texas, 2017) 1:28

32 https://www.psychologytoday.com/basics/cognitive-dissonance

33 Romans 7:15-23 New International Version

34 Dr. Stephen E. Bruneau "Iceberg Facts" http://www.icebergfinder.com/iceberg-facts.aspx (accessed 27 January 2018)

35 Claudio Fernandez-Araoz, Andrew Roscoe and Kentaro Aramaki, *"Turning Potential into Success: the Missing Link in Leadership Development"*, Harvard Business Review, Nov/Dec 2017, 86

36 Epictetus, philosopher https://www.brainyquote.com/quotes/epictetus_384454

37 1 Corinthians: 13:12 (New International Version)

38 *Brainyquote.com, "Stephen Jay Gould"*
https://www.brainyquote.com/quotes/stephen_jay_gould_164544
(accessed 28 Jan. 2018)

39 Barbara Fittipaldi, Pat Barrentine, ed., *When the Canary Stops
Singing: Women's Perspectives on Transforming Business*, (San Francisco:
Berrett-Koehler Publishers, Inc. 1993), 224

40 2 Corinthians 10:3-6 (New International Version)

41 Mark 4:23-25 (New International Version)

42 Barbara Fittipaldi, Pat Barrentine, ed., *When the Canary Stops
Singing: Women's Perspectives on Transforming Business*, (San Francisco:
Berrett-Koehler Publishers, Inc. 1993), 228

43 1 Corinthians 9:19-23 (New King James Version)

44 James Dao and Thom Shankar, "No Longer a Soldier, Shinseki Has a
New Mission", The New York Times, 10 Nov. 2009,
http://www.nytimes.com/2009/11/11/us/politics/11vets.html

45 *Brainyquote.com*, Simon Sinek"
https://www.brainyquote.com/search_results?q=One+of+the+best+para-
doxes+of+leadership+is+a+leader%E2%80%99s+need+to+be+both+stub-
born+a (accessed 28 Jan. 2018)

46 Daniel Pink TEDGlobal 2009,
https://www.ted.com/talks/dan_pink_on_motivation/transcript, 12:17

47 Proverbs 29:18 (King James Version)

48 1 Corinthians 9:24-27 (New International Version)

49 Thoughtco.com, "Hugh Elliott" https://www.thoughtco.com/inspir-

ing-quotes-about-miracles-124312 (accessed 28 Jan. 2018)

50 Galatians 6:4-5 (The Message translation of the Bible by Eugene Peterson)

51 1 Corinthians 10:12-14 (New King James Version)

52 Ryan Holiday, *The Obstacle is the Way* (New York: Penguin Group, 2014), 177

53 Peter Senge, C. Otto Scharmer, Joseph Jaworski and Betty Sue Flowers, *Presence: Human Purpose and the Field of the Future* (Cambridge: The Society for Organizational Learning, Inc., 2004), 132

54 Charles Spurgeon, *According to Promise*, (New York: Funk & Wagnalls, 1887), 50

55 Malcolm Gladwell, *Outliers: The Story of Success*, (New York: Little, Brown and Company, 2008), 194

56 https://leadershipfreak.blog/2014/01/22/jack-welch-grabbed-jim-mccann-by-the-collar/

57 Douglas Stone, Bruce M. Patton and Sheila Heen, *Difficult Conversations: How to Discuss What Matters Most* (New York: Viking Penguin, 1999), derived from Chapter 3

58 Douglas Stone, Bruce M. Patton and Sheila Heen, *Difficult Conversations: How to Discuss What Matters Most* (New York: Viking Penguin, 1999), 46

59 Susan Scott, *Fierce Conversations: Achieving Success at Work and in Life One Conversation at a Time* (New York: Berkley, 2002), 10.

60 Robert C. Solomon and Fernando Flores, *Building Trust: in Business, Politics, Relationships, and Life* (New York: Oxford University Press, Inc., 2001), 4.

61 Brennan Manning, *Abba's Child: the Cry of the Heart for Intimate Belonging* (Colorado Springs: NavPress, 1994), 146

62 Matthew 6:14-15 (New International Version)

63 Henri Nouwen, *You Are the Beloved: Daily Meditations for Spiritual Living,* (New York: Crown Publishing Group, 2017), 264

64 Edwin H. Friedman, *A Failure of Nerve: Leadership in the Age of the Quick Fix,* (New York: Church Publishing Inc., 2007) Preface.

65 Henri J. M. Nouwen, *Here and Now* (New York: Crossroad Publishing Company, 1994), 93

66 https://www.theguardian.com/science/2014/dcc/16/cognitive-benefits-handwriting-decline-typing

67 *Goodreads.com, "Benjamin Franklin",* https://www.goodreads.com/quotes/search?utf8=%E2%9C%93&q=Hide+not+your+talents%2C+they+for+use+were+made.+What%27s+a+sundial+in+the+shade&commit=Search (accessed 28 Jan. 2018)

68 Timothy Ferris, *Tools of Titans: The Tactics, Routines, and Habits of Billionaires, Icons, and World-Class Performers,* (New York: Houghton Mifflin Harcourt Publishing Company, 2017), 507

69 *Goodreads.com, "Albert Camus",* https://www.goodreads.com/quotes/6485-real-generosity-towards-the-future-lies-in-giving-all-to (accessed 28 Jan. 2018)

70 Rumi, translation by Coleman Barks, *The Essential Rumi* (New York: Harper Collins Publishers, 2003), 246

71 Rosamund Stone Zander and Benjamin Zander, *The Art of Possibility: Transforming Professional and Personal Life* (Boston: Harvard Business School Press, 2000), 126

72 G. K. Chesterton, *Chesterton Day by Day*, edited by Michael Parry, (Seattle: Inkling Books, 2002), 7